CINCINNATI

The Bicentennial Year in Review

Our Bicentennial will take its place in history as a year full of wonderful memories for every Greater Cincinnatian. Each spectacular event thrilled the crowds with colorful pageantry. The arts and educational programs engaged area residents of all ages in discoveries about their unique heritage. The capital improvement projects gave the community a sense of accomplishment and civic pride.

The Bicentennial evoked so many diverse feelings for each of us, it would be impossible to describe them all. Fortunately, this publication comes close. The photographs and captions were chosen carefully to recall the emotion of 1988.

We have assembled the most able group of professionals in Cincinnati to produce "Celebrate '88: The Bicentennial Year in Review". A team of award-winning photographers was selected to capture the many facets of the celebration. The graphic design is our own Bicentennial "look" and reflects the excitement of this year. The editor has written almost every word about the Bicentennial for the Commission since it was formed. The publisher is a trusted name in Cincinnati.

We know you will like the result of this collaboration as much as we do. The book embraces the dynamic spirit of this great city at its finest moment, and gives you the chance to enjoy and to share that moment in history for years to come.

◆

Joseph S. Stern, Jr.
Chairman
Greater Cincinnati Bicentennial Commission

◆

Richard J. Greiwe
Executive Director
Greater Cincinnati Bicentennial Commission

Design Directors
Steven Dulle
Kelly Kolar

Designers
Steven Dulle
Kelly Kolar
Braddly Bush
Laura Martin

Editor
Mary Lynn Ricks

**Official Bicentennial
Photographers**
Hal Barkan
Michael Bennington
Bicentennial Archives
Robert A. Flischel
Maureen France
Jeff Friedman
Bob Gerrior
William Hudson
John Keeling
Brad Smith
Chris Taggart
Tony Walsh
J. Miles Wolf

Typesetting
Graphitti Studios

Printing
Young & Klein, Inc.

ISBN 0-9608016-6-9
Printed in the United States
of America by
Young & Klein, Inc.
1351 Spring Lawn Avenue
Cincinnati, Ohio 45223

First Edition

CONTENTS

INTRODUCTION

What a glorious year! From the dawn of our bicentennial to its climactic close, 1988 is sure to be remembered – by those who experienced it and those who will come to know about it – as Greater Cincinnati's finest hour. A year when civic pride was at its zenith. A year when people from throughout the nation and the world visited our city and discovered its old world charm and new world excitement. A year when an unprecedented number of regional, national and international reporters covered stories about what our city was doing to celebrate its 200th birthday. A year when pigs were kings and a jovial-looking man named Cincinnatus stole the hearts of thousands of children.

As the memories begin to settle in our minds, and we begin to remember the year as a whole instead of its separate pieces, the question arises, "How was it all done?" For certainly, much more was accomplished than even the most active imaginations could envision. What led up to the sterling successes of 1988 was an unshaking perseverance and a lot of hard work that took the Commission on many different pathways heading toward one main purpose: to plan and implement a celebration worthy of the historic significance of Cincinnati's 200th birthday.

So, where did it begin? In July, 1982, then Mayor David Mann called upon City Council to adopt a resolution calling for the formation of a commission of civic-minded individuals representing all facets of our community. This body of people would have the responsibility of planning and implementing a fitting commemoration of Greater Cincinnati's bicentennial.

The resolution was not a verbose document with vague descriptions of what could occur. Rather, it set forth a specific set of goals against which the commission would be measured: 1) to establish a permanent legacy of the celebration, 2) to attract regional visitors and enhance the city's national image, and 3) to involve every Greater Cincinnatian in the planned activities.

Think about those for a moment. Individually they represent a very tall order, but collectively they seem relatively impossible. And yet, think of the events which occurred during the bicentennial year. Amazingly, the Greater Cincinnati Bicentennial Commission was able to go before City Council in early 1989 and report that indeed it had met the mandate set forth more than six years before. Its remarkable list of successes makes it one of the most effective and efficient commissions in our city's history.

Initially, 15 men and women were selected in late 1982 to serve, on a volunteer basis, as Bicentennial Commissioners. Chaired by Joseph S. Stern, Jr., the Commission was comprised of persons from all walks of life who shared a common love of their city. They met in a small room in City Hall on a quarterly basis and began to map out the what's and how's of meeting the challenges before them. As the years progressed, City Council appointed additional persons to serve on the Commission. By 1988, there were 38 members.

The first order of business on the Commission's agenda in 1983 was to select a person to serve as its executive director. Notifications were placed in the newspapers and resumes began clogging City Hall mailboxes. In November, Richard J. Greiwe, a fifth-generation Cincinnatian, was elected to this enviable position.

The second agenda item was to establish a corporate identity for the newly-formed Commission. Artists from throughout the Greater Cincinnati area entered their concept of the perfect logo. Some celebrated our ties to the Ohio River, others highlighted the surrounding hills, some were very stylized and futuristic while others were classical with simple elegance.

But it was the design of intertwined 88s by William Sontag which captured the prize. The two eights signified the year, and copy above and below identified our city and established 1988 as our 200th birthday. Sontag's design was a perfectly simple way to communicate the Commission's identity and purpose. It

1 9 8 2

1 9 8 3

would be impossible to guess the number and variety of visual mediums on which that graphic has appeared...from stationery to event sweatshirts to carpeting for a parade.

In January, Greiwe opened an office in Room 138 of City Hall. The space, furnishings and telephone were all donated. In addition, The Greater Cincinnati Foundation had issued a $30,000 grant to get the Commission started. In February, the first employee was hired and two volunteers agreed to work several days each week. The staff was assembled and work was begun.

Since there are no textbooks on how to plan a 200th birthday celebration, intensive research was initiated into the activities of other cities celebrating similar events. Boston, Philadelphia, Toronto and Los Angeles were some of the cities contacted, and much was learned. Ideas were collected on how to highlight the arts, involve children and senior citizens, create national attention, raise the necessary funding and just plain have fun. What other cities had done provided a guideline, but the calendar of activities for Cincinnati's bicentennial would have to come from its people.

In February, news releases were sent to the general media calling for citizens to share their dreams for this special year. A simple enough request, one might think. But it generated tremendously creative ideas.

The Commission received a diversity of suggestions from all ages. Construct a monumental totem sculpture illustrating our city's history. Develop Sawyer Point into a recreational facility. Bring the Price Hill incline back to life. Create a museum complex blending the greatest attributes of the nation's natural and social history, science and children's museum centers.

To determine the feasibility and appropriateness of the ideas sent to the Commission, the Legacy Committee was formed to study "bricks and mortar" projects which would be a lasting legacy of our bicentennial celebration.

Soon after, seven volunteer advisory committees (Arts, Education, History, River Events, Downtown Events, Community Coordination and Northern Kentucky) began to formulate substantive proposals for those programs approved by a Goals & Mission Committee. It was during this year and by these inaugural committees that the framework of the year-long calendar was produced. The major celebrations were outlined, and a direction for arts, education and community programs was discussed.

In March, the Commission held a news conference to announce 60 of the citizen proposals which were under consideration. By early summer, that list had been pared to seven by the Legacy Committee and a brochure entitled "Dreams Fit for a Queen" was produced to publicize these potential birthday presents. At the same time, a slide presentation was prepared to introduce the community to the extravagant Centennial commemorative activities, share the research gleaned from other cities' celebrations, and put forth a community challenge to prepare for an unparalleled year.

Together, the slide presentation and brochure were presented to literally hundreds of organizations and community meetings by Greiwe and members of the Bicentennial Speakers Bureau, formed that summer to spread the word and invite the participation of all in the planning of this historic occasion.

Some of the original dreams in that simple brochure were never realized. One called for *The President,* a grand riverboat built here in 1925, to be brought back to Cincinnati and renovated into a floating restaurant and entertainment center. Ironically, *The President* visited Cincinnati during Tall Stacks and commanded the longest lines and greatest interest of all the participating riverboats.

But to the Commission's credit, 4 of the 7 ideas have been initiated as bicentennial projects: development of a riverfront recreational facility at Sawyer Point, improvements to Eggleston Avenue, creation of a Museum Center and construction of a tram connecting Mt. Adams to the downtown central district.

City officials and corporate leaders made known their choice amongst the ideas presented in the brochure. Development of the riverfront was a priority agenda item. For more than a decade, various committees of architects and planners had been pushing for implementation of a design plan created in the early 1970s. The story began in 1972 with a Christmas Eve telephone call from the late Charles Sawyer to Ewart "Sink" Simpkinson, a strong proponent of riverfront development.

Sawyer's message was short but powerful – he would donate $1 million which would be matched by a federal Land & Conservation Grant to allow the City to purchase and clear the acreage that came to be known as Sawyer Point. It was a scrap metal junk yard, a blighted expanse of prime property that stood at Cincinnati's doorstep.

A family-oriented recreational center was the City's goal for these 22 acres. To promote the design plan, a three-dimensional model was constructed, illustrating the architects' translation of that goal. Tennis courts, a fishing pier, river overlooks, an adventure play area for children, a promenade for arts and crafts festivals, a performance pavilion with an expansive area of grass to provide natural seating...these were the major elements of the Sawyer Point design.

But the necessary dollars to transform the land into a family gathering place were not forthcoming, even a decade later. And so the City looked to Cincinnati's 200th birthday as a viable deadline to move this project from the drawing table and into the construction stages.

Enter the Bicentennial Commission. It seemed a foregone conclusion that the Commission would set its fund-raising sights on Sawyer Point. The bicentennial was a powerful catalyst to energize large and small business interests, and the Commission offered the synergy to get the job done. But in 1984, the Commission was not yet ready to commit...the creation of a Museum Center would also be a lasting legacy of the bicentennial.

In addition to the discussion surrounding these capital improvement projects, a constant stream of citizen-initiated program ideas was finding its way across the desktops and in the conversations of Commission staff each day. One was the lighting of the John A. Roebling Suspension Bridge, the forerunner to the Brooklyn Bridge, built by the same man. The Commission agreed to establish a maintenance fund for the bridge lighting. During Riverfest, 1984, the lighting ceremony was held. A brilliant photograph taken that evening was used for a poster produced and sold through the Commission with the theme, "Lighting the Way to '88...Our Bicentennial Year."

To keep the 400 committee members, volunteers, and business and civic leaders involved in bicentennial planning informed of the Commission's ongoing progress, a newsletter was initiated in October. When the final issue was mailed in December of 1988, the newsletter was being sent to close to 6,000 individuals and businesses.

A sizeable gift was presented to the Commission in January of 1985 when the American Society of Landscape Architects (ASLA) announced the donation of a design plan to transform the narrow, potholed Eggleston Avenue into a grand boulevard. Eggleston provided the most direct access from downtown to the riverfront, and therefore its improvement became an important consideration.

In March, the Commission voted officially to adopt Bicentennial Commons at Sawyer Point as its legacy project, and the major thrust of its fund-raising efforts. Soon after, a lead gift of $2 million was announced by The Procter & Gamble Company. While the Commission was in complete support of the original concept behind the development, it did question the current status of some of the design elements. Almost 15 years earlier when the plan was unveiled, it was considered avant-garde. But the 1990s would demand something quite different.

The Commission looked across the country at what was presently considered

on the cutting edge of "public places" design. In response to this research, several additional elements were presented to the City for consideration. They included 1) a revolutionary ice/roller skating surface, 2) construction of a historic walkway connecting the riverfronts of Cincinnati, Covington and Newport, 3) a geologic timeline, 4) a family-style restaurant located in a boat house training facility for Olympic-bound rowers, 5) volleyball courts, 6) an expansive entrance sculpture using water as a medium, 7) construction of river overlooks atop the L & N Arches, and 8) a miniature golf course using Greater Cincinnati area landmarks as the theme for each of the 18 holes.

Each new element added to the preliminary $12 million cost of the facility, but Commissioners felt strongly about the importance of these innovative additions. A walk through Bicentennial Commons today is proof positive, with the only deletion being the golf course, replaced by an exercise pars course.

In July, the Commission and the Cincinnati Recreation Commission arranged for a test area of the revolutionary skating surface called "glice" to be flown to Cincinnati. Skating club members and local officials and dignitaries donned ice or roller skates to give the surface their toughest test. By the end of the day, glice was proclaimed perfect.

In September, the plans for Eggleston Avenue were unveiled. Of course, monies from the City were needed to implement the plan, and property owners along Eggleston were called upon to become "partners" in the project in that they would assist in the maintenance of the landscaping. Repaving and widening the roadway were undertaken by the City to connect Bicentennial Commons to the heart of downtown.

So it was smooth sailing for the Commission as it initiated its fund-raising campaign in October of 1985. In preparation, one-page descriptions and budgets for each project, program and event were compiled. A booklet, loosely titled the "ideal bicentennial year," was also produced. And although it was the product of vivid imaginations when written, most of what was presented within came to be.

On the booklet's cover, a community challenge was put forth: "We are at the threshold of an event which takes place only once...our bicentennial year. The fact that it takes place in our lifetime is a privilege we must respect and a challenge we must embrace." And so, the campaign began.

As opposed to a general collection of funds then to be allocated by the Commission, the fund-raising campaign was structured to allow funding prospects to select a program, project or event to underwrite. This strategy instilled in contributors a feeling of ownership, a true sense of pride in the success of their endeavor.

Funding levels were established designating Official Sponsors ($200,000 and above), Proud Patrons ($25,000 to $199,999), Contributors ($5,000 to $24,999), Friends (under $5,000) and Suppliers ($10,000 and above in goods and services).

Corporations, foundations, small businesses and individuals were contacted. More than 500 personal campaign calls were made by members of the Steering Committee during late 1985 and 1986. And hundreds of letters and booklets were mailed to addresses in downtown and the far corners of the region.

In all, 1,500 companies contributed to the bicentennial celebration. The list of supporters is an inspiring mixture of international corporations, small businesses and dedicated individuals. It is a shining example of the cooperative spirit which has nurtured this city's growth for the past 200 years, and will continue to chart a path of progress for Cincinnati's third century.

Support for the bicentennial was seen on both sides of the Ohio River. In the fall, the Northern Kentucky Steering Committee selected the Riverwalk through Covington and Newport as the focus of its fund-raising efforts, ensuring the completion of this educational and entertaining pathway of our history. This Committee had been formed with the conviction that combining the resources of the entire region would lead to an even greater celebration. The Riverwalk epitomized that conviction. It encircled the two shores, drawing residents of Cincinnati and Northern Kentucky closer together in the sharing of their mutual heritage.

Plans for the Riverwalk called for 36 historic elements, or stations, to be located along a 4-mile walkway through Bicentennial Commons, Riverside Drive and Taylor Park. It was an ambitious and comprehensive project. One of its most captivating elements was the construction of 7 life-size sculptures to be placed along Riverside Drive, each depicting a historic personality associated with the river. Even as design efforts were getting underway, the project was heralded as one of the most impressive American statuary collections of the 20th century.

While the Commission's fund-raising efforts got underway and the legacy projects moved forward, the Commission took a step in the design direction. Noting the incredible publicity centered on the work of architects and graphic designers involved in the 1984 Olympics in Los Angeles, the Commission looked to the people and theories which gave birth to this phenomenon.

One fact became very clear: it was imperative that a consistent, understandable and festive graphic design system be applied to all signage, merchandise, printed and promotional materials and venue decoration. The success of the L.A. Olympics lit a Cincinnati spark that soon grew into a flame which resulted in the bicentennial graphic design system.

Similar research led to a workshop that highlighted the importance of creating a "city identity" – a polishing and packaging of unique characteristics – that could be achieved by enhancing the natural beauty and ambiance of a city. Local architects and graphic designers were taken on a series of walks during the workshop where Cincinnati's potential as a tourism destination was uncovered. Again a flame was ignited, leading to the development of a City Identity Program proposal for Cincinnati, and the Commission began a search for funds.

An effective tool in creating bicentennial funding fever was the bi-weekly placement of advertisements in a local business publication highlighting those companies which contributed $10,000 or more to the Commission. The announcements were entitled, "Invest in our Third Century," and the exposure within the business community was so great that the Commission began receiving inquiries from companies as to how they could be featured in an upcoming issue. The answer was simple! Later in the year, the same theme was transferred to video for 30-second spots which ran during early morning news programs.

A most appreciated surge of funding came to the Commission's doorstep in separate news conferences held in late February and early March. A bipartisan partnership of state elected officials led by Governor Richard Celeste announced two separate grants to boost bicentennial legacy projects.

First it was revealed that $8 million in the State's capital improvements budget was targeted for the renovation of Union Terminal into a museum complex. The grant was contingent upon the passage of a May 6, 1986 tax levy of $41.7 million. In February, the Commission voted to endorse the public tax levy and assigned members to serve as public spokespersons for the museum center project. Supporters gathered at Union Terminal to watch election returns finally received victorious news late in the night.

Just a few weeks later, the Governor announced a $4 million economic development grant to the City for the construction of the Mt. Adams Tram. From its inception, the tram met with some resistance among the hill's residents, but proponents stated it would enhance the visitor attractions in both Mt. Adams and downtown by providing a more direct route between the two.

With the dissolution of the Commission, the future of the tram rests with the City's Economic Development Department which continues to work toward the acquisition of air rights, the property for landing terminals and adequate insurance.

Also in the spring, the Commission held a public competition to create the

1 9 8 6

"look" for the bicentennial. In May, the Bicentennial Design Collaborative, a team of students and instructors from the University of Cincinnati's School of Design, Architecture, Art and Planning, was chosen. They created a design system consisting of a vibrant color palette (bright blue, bronze, purple, burgundy, teal, peach, orange and yellow), pictograms (graphic images depicting regional landmarks), a torn edge (depicting Cincinnati's hilly terrain), use of a pattern and Univers typography.

A Design Standards Guide was published later in the year and distributed to contributors and their advertising agencies encouraging them to incorporate the bicentennial "look" into promotional and merchandising materials.

All bicentennial publications, merchandise, promotional materials and venue design would reflect the design system created from this immensely talented group of students. Suddenly, new words like "pictogram," "sonotube," "architrave" and "venue" crept into the Commission's vocabulary.

And it worked! In fact, the bicentennial design system is so popular that its components have found their way onto printed and published materials beyond the Commission's realm, and it is safe to say its influence will last for many years.

A more tangible lasting legacy got underway in the fall when the bulldozers headed for Bicentennial Commons to ready the grounds for construction of the facilities. They had a concrete deadline to meet…the Dedication was set for June 4th and 5th, 1988. A somewhat unexpected problem crews encountered was the number of interested citizens who visited the site to watch this dream unfold!

Summer found the Commission involved in another public competition and embroiled in its first real controversy, over an impish little fellow whose name was Cincinnatus. Area artists were invited to submit their ideas for the bicentennial mascot. A white tiger, a cheese coney, a pig, a caricature of a royal lady named Queen Cydie, a German in lederhosen and a riverboat captain were among the entries.

Four finalists were printed in mid-August editions of the Saturday and Sunday daily papers. The public was asked to vote for their favorite, and the rendering of Cincinnatus won. It seemed an appropriate choice, for he is our namesake. But somewhere along the way some residents confused mascot with logo, and bicentennial with city. They feared this little man would begin appearing on the mayor's stationery and the city seal.

No, the Commission tried to explain, but not before numerous television, radio and newspaper reporters did seemingly hundreds of interviews. Finally, spirits calmed and Cincinnatians came to understand that the mascot's role was just like Mickey Mouse at Disneyland.

And still the Commission ventured on another public voting mission, this time to choose the major "neighborhood" program for the bicentennial year. A comprehensive survey was sent in the fall to over 400 neighborhood, village, township and city councils in the Greater Cincinnati area. Results of the questionnaire would determine the most widely accepted community program for which the Commission would then raise funds.

An even larger mailing went out in November to 7,000 small businesses. The square, orange brochure called "The Birthday Book" invited these companies to buy a present for Cincinnati's birthday. The suggested gifts were elements of the City Identity Program, and the "The Birthday Book" was the Commission's answer to funding this expansive proposal. Price tags were listed next to each item. Landscaping at gateway entrances to the city was $30,000 per site. Downtown flower baskets at $125 each. The gift list was varied and contributions came in, even from the 4th grade class at Carthage School.

In the fall, the rusting railroad trestle at the entrance of Sawyer Point was removed. Months of negotiations and fund-seeking finally paid off for the Commission, whose plans for a grand entranceway sculpture for the recreational facility were stymied until the trestle was removed.

And a final boost to take the Commission into a new year came from Xavier University's School of Business, which developed a business plan for the Commission and agreed to conduct an economic impact study to determine the effect of special events on the city's economy. City, tourism and Commission officials all looked to 1988 as a test. Would the public celebrations being planned by the Commission really show a marked increase in visitors to the city?

The Commission insisted the answer was yes, and set its sights on the last year of planning to make its prediction ring true.

As the Commission moved into 1987, it moved into new office space in the Chiquita Center. With an expanded staff, and more to come, Room 138 in City Hall had become cramped quarters. By the middle of the year, there were 13 full-time staff members and the same number of office volunteers on staggered schedules. So, even the new space three times the size of the old was filled quickly.

Another change occurred, that being a shift from planning and fund-raising to implementation and publicity. Through the previous years, most of the Commission's communication efforts were directed to corporate contributors and volunteers through the newsletter and annual reports. But the World Figure Skating Championships held in Cincinnati in March would attract national and international media.

To inform this captive audience of bicentennial activities, a calendar of events brochure and travelling display were produced. This tandem effort resulted in the promotion of not only Commission-sponsored events but also major, community-wide activities such as the Australian koala visit at the Cincinnati Zoo. The seed was planted for future publicity efforts.

In April, it was announced that Andrew Leicester's design of an environmental sculpture was selected for the entrance to Bicentennial Commons at Sawyer Point, the name officially given the riverfront recreational complex by the Commission. Leicester's environmental sculpture, later named Cincinnati Gateway, was 300' long and 50' wide with 17 separate historical symbols, including a canal lock, a miniature Ohio River, a 100' flood column and four pigs with wings, a whimsical tribute to Cincinnati's days as Porkopolis. The sculpture design was accepted by all, heralded as one of the most thrilling art works dedicated in Cincinnati.

Just six months later, Leicester was being interviewed by a newspaper reporter and began to describe the details of his sculpture, centering on the four smokestacks, atop which would be red pigs with wings. His words were full of imagery and so intense was his description of these pigs that it comprised the first half of the news story, which appeared on the front page.

By 10:00 a.m., the Commission phones were ringing off the hook. How could money be spent on this "pig on a stick"? Never mind that these porcine pets were only 1/17th of the sculpture. In letters to the editors and letters to the mayor's office, the Commission was asked to halt the construction process and look for something more appropriate. It became an issue of national intrigue as the controversy was heading toward a confrontation testing the sanctity of public art.

The debate culminated in a public hearing in Council chambers. The place was packed with "Pro Art" and "Save the Pigs" banners waving. As it turned out, the public hearing was a moot point as one of the first to speak was a City attorney who reminded Council the sculpture had been reviewed and accepted months before! But all was not lost. The publicity surrounding the winged pigs made them the most popular merchandise and promotional design in the city. Cincinnati had, at least in spirit, returned to the days of Porkopolis.

A less publicized generator of phone calls to the Commission office was the Bicentennial Bricks which went on sale in August of 1987. These personalized bricks would pave walkways in Bicentennial Commons, Riverside Drive and

Taylor Park. Thirty-five thousand people stepped into history through the campaign, which offered an unexpected challenge to purchasers: finding their brick.

People were getting dizzy walking up and down the many rows with their heads bent forward. So, the Commission held a series of brick-finder weekends in September of 1988 and assisted hundreds of purchasers in locating their piece of history. The more adventuresome souls are determined to find their brick unaided, and can still be seen walking slowly back and forth, row after row!

In the fall, the Commission celebrated the groundbreaking of the Boat House, located just east of Bicentennial Commons. The Boat House was a concept introduced to the City in 1986 by the Commission with direction and support from local rowing enthusiasts. With a family restaurant on the upper level and a state-of-the-art fitness center and rowing training facility on the ground level, the Boat House provides another year-round attraction to the riverfront.

But the real activity in the Commission office was centered on the first event, The Countdown, just three months away.

The Events Steering Committee, a volunteer group of City officials, insurance and publicity experts and volunteer coordination staff, was formed to handle the nuts and bolts of planning events of this magnitude. Weekly meetings throughout the next year and one-half addressed the major issues and minute details of throwing a party for anywhere from tens of thousands to 1 million people.

To provide corporate contributors with a preview of each of the events, premiere parties were planned by a creative group of volunteers serving on the Hospitality Committee.

Brightly decorated welcome kits were readied for special visitors to the city. Twenty thousand kits were placed in downtown hotel rooms during selected bicentennial events. They included a pocket map, dining guide, coupons for Cincinnati taste treats, a party horn, confetti and a greeting card.

Design plans were also finalized for the Bicentennial Reception Center in The Westin Atrium. Centrally located, the Center publicized bicentennial activities and featured weekly changing exhibits on local companies and organizations. Visitors were welcomed by bicentennial greeters at the Center from April through October.

A much larger effort to inform people of Cincinnati's bicentennial involved the contributions of local advertising agencies, public relations firms, radio and television stations and newspapers. One agency was selected to develop advertising materials for each of the five major events. In addition, the public relations firms contributed services to spread the bicentennial word to regional, national and international audiences.

Local radio and television stations and the newspapers were more than generous in donating prime air time to publicize bicentennial activities throughout 1988. And each event was televised live to share the celebration with those unable to attend.

There was even a song written to publicize bicentennial events. "Celebrate '88" was recorded by a celebrity chorus featuring local newscasters, musicians and government officials.

For residents who missed all of the above, there was the bicentennial info line; 352-1988 offered up-to-the-minute details on all bicentennial happenings.

In October, the Commission strutted its stuff with a gala kickoff to the bicentennial year. A recognition award was presented to contributors and volunteers, and 1988 previews were displayed offering a peek at what was to come. With the sudden blast of a confetti cannon, Cincinnatus made his public debut and was an immediate star. Before the evening ended, he had posed for 100 photographs with the founding members of his fan club!

During that same period, the official bicentennial commemorative medal made its debut in gold, silver and bronze. With the "Genius of Water" on the front, and a representation of Ft. Washington and today's riverfront on the back, the medal became a treasured keepsake of this historic observance. Stores were also flooded with a wide range of bicentennial merchandise. Consumers were warned to look for the "88" logo to ensure they were purchasing official products.

It seemed before anyone realized, it was the morning of December 31, 1987. The Commission stood poised to greet the bicentennial year, to welcome it with open arms for all the trials and tribulations, the tears and the cheers it would surely present. The atmosphere in the office that day, in fact that whole month, was electrifying. Anxiety. Anticipation. Excitement. It was all there between staff members and volunteers exhausted and exhilarated.

From the first minute of The Countdown to the final seconds of The Bicentennial Birthday, 1988 was the ultimate rollercoaster ride. Perfect, except that it ended all too quickly.

In many ways, it was hard for Commissioners staff members and volunteers to say good-bye to the bicentennial and to each other. They had worked as a close family, and together had produced an impressive list of accomplishments:

- ◆ $65 million in capital improvements initiated as bicentennial projects
  - Bicentennial Commons at Sawyer Point
  - Riverwalk
  - The Boat House
  - Eggleston Esplanade
  - Museum Center at Union Terminal
  - Mt. Adams Tram
- ◆ $2 million raised to produce five nationally-recognized events
- ◆ Event attendance record set of 1.9 million people throughout 1988
- ◆ Bicentennial events generated an estimated $70 million in economic impact on the community
- ◆ $17 million worth of publicity generated through print and electronic media coverage of the bicentennial year
- ◆ 153 million people reached with bicentennial publicity
- ◆ 350 regional and national reporters covered bicentennial events
- ◆ Tall Stacks named "One of the Top Ten Events in the World" by the *Toronto Globe & Mail*
- ◆ Cincinnati named one of the "in" cities for 1989 in a poll reported in *The New York Times*
- ◆ In just one year, Cincinnati moved from 104th to 31st position in *Money Magazine's* 1989 survey of the nation's best places to live
- ◆ $1 million raised for arts, education and community programs with an estimated 500,000 Greater Cincinnatians participating
- ◆ 1,500 Greater Cincinnati corporations, foundations and organizations contributed cash, goods or services
- ◆ 5,000 residents served as volunteers at the five major events
- ◆ 700 residents served on program planning committees

Each page that follows shares a fascinating chapter in the story of the bicentennial year. Breathtaking photography captures unforgettable images. Hopefully, personal memories will shared so that the spirit of the bicentennial celebration, what it meant to each person who witnessed its glory, will live on through the next one hundred years.

1 9 8 8

THE COUNTDOWN

It dawned grey and cold with drizzling rain. The weatherman promised no improvement for the most important day in the Bicentennial Commission's history. December 31, 1987. The Countdown. The beginning. The test.

Would it be the extraordinary event that carefree imaginations of an entire city had been dreaming of for four years? It had to be, because "firsts" are so important, and The Countdown was the first event. It would have to meet, and hopefully exceed, the highest expectations of residents, contributors and city officials. Or, as Commission Chairman Joseph S. Stern, Jr. would say, "It has to knock the socks off a rooster."

But there were no rays of sunshine promising success, except those in the hearts and hard-working bodies of 700 volunteers, a dozen staff members and more than 60 performance groups determined to make this very special New Year's Eve incomparable. And so it was.

Beginning at 4:00 p.m. when the Children's Festival filled The Westin Hotel Atrium, The Countdown was packed with people. From the eastern end of the Skywalk to the far west corners of the Convention Center, 27 stages were set to showcase the talents of musicians, artists, dancers, singers, actors, puppeteers and mimes who played to capacity crowds from afternoon until early morning. The Countdown was a kaleidoscope of sight and sound, an unrelenting progression of one good thing after another. The city's pulse was racing.

Countdown Admission Button sales were limited to 30,000 due to safety concerns. But as the evening progressed, the crowds increased as residents headed downtown to participate in the Fountain Square finale, open to the public.

So rampant was the energy and activity of New Year's Eve revelers that 11:50 p.m. – the countdown to midnight – came all too quickly. A crowd of 60,000 processed to Fountain Square, spilling out into the street and along the sidewalks. And there, the youthful spirit of the Bicentennial surged forth in a blaze of excitement: pulsating music, fanciful lasers, colorful beams of light and historic images splashed upon the building sides mezmerized the crowd and produced an unforgettable ten minutes in our city's history.

The final ten seconds were serenaded by hoarse voices, each straining to make its mark upon this historic occasion. "10-9-8-7-6-5-4-3-2-1 Happy New Year!!!" A sudden burst of fireworks exploded to create a rousing welcome to our Bicentennial year.

Although the weather remained uncooperative throughout the night, The Countdown was a smashing success. So much so that public demand has made it a Cincinnati New Year's Eve tradition.

DECEMBER 31, 1987

Look out, rooster!

Installing the 22′ × 33′ screen for the finale on Fountain Square proved to be quite a feat. A Water Works crane was used to hoist it into position, but not before engineering studies were made to determine if the weight of the crane would damage this historic landmark.

It took a week to build all the scaffolding and install the necessary equipment for the finale. For the laser show alone, 20 mirrors were secured to the stage and to locations along the perimeter of the Square. Since moisture intensifies the effects of lasers, the intermittent rain throughout the day and evening was quite beneficial.

A near-midnight rehearsal December 30, 1987 ended with a spontaneous round of applause from the small group of Commission and WCPO-TV9 staff members gathered on Fountain Square. The desired effect had been achieved, even for those who had been involved in the planning of this inaugural event for so many years. Channel 9 aired The Countdown live, sharing the excitement of this Bicentennial premiere with all residents.

tock   **tick**   tock   tick   tock   tock

tick   tock   tock   tick   **tock**   tick   tock

tick   tock   **tick**

tick   tock   tock

tick   **tock**

tick

The Atrium of The Westin Hotel came alive with the smiles and laughter of thousands of children entranced with the talents of clowns, puppeteers and jugglers. Almost everyone at the Children's Festival became friends with "Honey," the lovable and unpredictable monkey who accompanied organ grinder Jim McCune.

tick

tock

tick

Sixty diverse performance groups entertained from 27 venues spread across the Skywalk system and in hotel lobbies and the Convention Center. From mimes to lumberjacks, the crowds responded with enthusiastic applause. Of course the latter did leave a bit more of a mess to clear. According to the clean-up crew, it looked like beavers had invaded the Convention Place Mall. All in all, Cincinnati's rich cultural heritage was celebrated in grand style.

tick   tock

The Convention Center rocked and rolled with the sounds of Big Band to Motown. MTV was also there, spinning tunes and playing videos of the most popular groups. Capacity crowds dancing to the seven bands spread throughout the three levels had an unnerving effect on the floors – they started dancing, too. In response, Safety officials closed the Convention Center for several hours. But those inside kept the party going until 1:00 a.m.

tick

tock

By 11:30 p.m., Fountain Square was jammed with Countdowners dancing their way through the final minutes of the year. They were entertained with live music and Countdown broadcasts from WCPO-TV9 on a giant screen hanging from the stage. Finale host Gary Sandy, known best for his role as Andy Travis in the television series "WKRP in Cincinnati," kept the crowd revved up and ready to go during the half-hour show preceding the laser/light/music extravaganza.

12

Historic images flashed upon the Elder Beerman building during the Fountain Square finale were created by slides projected to the dimension of 120' × 80'. They told a story of our past, and how we progressed to this moment of celebration when we were about to welcome our 200th year. The slide of the Bicentennial "88" logo proclaimed the midnight hour.

Mayor Charles Luken, with wife Marcia, and Bicentennial Commission Chairman Joseph S. Stern, Jr., with wife Mary, pull the switch at 11:50 p.m. December 31, 1987 to begin the 10-minute laser/light/music extravaganza to count the minutes to midnight and the dawn of our Bicentennial year.

BONG

BONG

BONG BONG

BONG

THE DEDICATION

The beauty of spring, its colorful parade of blooming flowers and budding trees, painted a perfect setting for the June 3-5th dedication of one of America's most innovative riverfront developments.

Warm sunshine bathed the 350,000 people who came to inspect every inch of Bicentennial Commons at Sawyer Point. Opening ceremonies were designed to bring out the best from the east to the west end of this expansive recreational complex, and there were 1,350 volunteers on hand to make sure visitors experienced every detail.

From classical to contemporary, musical groups entertained thousands at the amphitheater, performance pavilion and stages set throughout the 22 acres. Families traveled through 440 million years as they walked along the geologic timeline. And fun-loving Cincinnatus posed for pictures with his friends at a most appropriate place – the bronze statue erected in honor of the real Lucius Quinctius Cincinnatus.

Ice- and roller-skating champions appearing at The Dedication gave a "thumbs up" to glice, the innovative surface on the year-round skating rink. Oscar Robertson and a host of local and nationally-known celebrities stirred up some hot matches to inaugurate the tennis courts. And a bit of California was brought in with the World Series of Women's Beach Volleyball Tournament to kick up some sand in the sand volleyball courts. Needless to say, these West Coast girls drew a large crowd of fans throughout the weekend.

Kid's Fest, held adjacent to Bicentennial Commons along Serpentine Wall, celebrated its 10th anniversary in splendid style, attracting thousands upon thousands of young citizens to an imaginative array of festivities.

Punctuating official dedication ceremonies at 12:00 noon on Saturday was the breathtaking demonstration by the U.S. Army Golden Knights. In complete synchronization, this team of expert parachutists fell through the sky to a precision landing near the pavilion stage. The last member carried the American flag and touched down in concert with the final notes of the Star-Spangled Banner…a very moving and patriotic moment for all.

Next to the immensely popular children's adventure playland, perhaps the most crowded area of Bicentennial Commons was the promenade, where personalized bricks had been laid. There was a constant stream of people walking back and forth, heads down, trying in earnest to find their bricks. There would be an occasional squeal of success, and in more than one instance, an embarrassed exchange between two searchers who bumped heads in their concentrated effort. Looking for bricks could be dangerous!

But, who can forget the true stars of this show – the internationally famous flying pigs. There they were, unveiled and in all their splendor, perched atop one of the nation's premiere environmental sculptures, standing guard in whimsical fashion. Whatever heated controversy had plagued their introduction into Cincinnati life, our porcine friends were now celebrities. They were the focal point of every photographer's lens.

In short, it was a banner weekend. Civic pride was soaring. In fact, the success of The Dedication and residents' appreciation of Bicentennial Commons can be encapsulated in the comments of a local television reporter who was quite disturbed that he could find no-one who had a complaint. His story wouldn't be balanced, he explained to a Commission staff member. "Sorry," she said, "but there is nothing I can do about that!"

JUNE 3 · 5, 1988

Up, up and away go hundreds of colorful balloons – biodegradable, of course – to signal the ribbon had been cut to officially dedicate Bicentennial Commons at Sawyer Point. It took nearly four hours to inflate the balloons, which were released by volunteers standing along the sides of the Performance Pavilion.

Ewart (Sink) Simpkinson saw his dream of over two decades come to reality with the dedication of Bicentennial Commons at Sawyer Point.

To play on the frenzied excitement surrounding the famous flying pigs, the U.S. Coast Guard was called in to put the finishing touch on the Cincinnati Gateway entrance sculpture. Sculpture supporters who gathered at these dedication ceremonies sported foam pigs-with-wings hats and wore shirts which read, "Because We Care There Are Pigs In The Air."

The 20 canal locks and dams located along the Ohio River from Pittsburgh, PA to Cairo, IL are represented by solid bronze markers, each weighing 50 pounds, which are spaced accurately along the miniature river atop the serpentine mound of Cincinnati Gateway.

This 300′ long, 50′ high environmental sculpture contains 17 historic elements which tell the story of Greater Cincinnati's geologic and social history.

A view from inside the Performance Pavilion illustrates the close proximity of Bicentennial Commons to downtown Cincinnati. This 22-acre riverfront recreational development stands as a legacy of our 200th birthday celebration, having been funded through the Commission by area corporations, businesses, foundations, individuals and governmental agencies. More than 1 million people took advantage of its wide range of year-round activities during 1988.

Fireworks had to be a part of The Dedication festivities. The special pyrotechnic effects to "burn" the Celebrate '88 message during the finale Sunday evening thrilled the crowd.

Sports of all sorts can be found at Bicentennial Commons. Sand volleyball and tennis were a big hit for the older set, while the under twelve group headed straight for the Adventure Play Area, complete with a bumpy blue slide. Volunteers from the Boy Scouts did an exceptional job of keeping this packed playground virtually safe and accident-free.

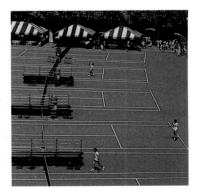

It is called "glice" and it is a revolutionary skating surface that will accept both ice and roller skates, providing year-round outdoor exercise and enjoyment. Developed in Belgium, Cincinnati is one of the first cities in America to experience its quality. And when one side wears down, the surface is simply turned over for years and years of fun.

1,350 volunteers did it all to make sure everyone discovered all the secrets of Bicentennial Commons.

Cincinnatus, the very popular Bicentennial mascot, finds an appropriate place to pose for photographs – in front of the bronze statue of his, and the city's, namesake. Cincinnatus braved the heat to say "hello" to all who came to The Dedication.

Look over there...is that really the Beatles? The Dedication was filled with surprises of music and merriment, keeping all the stage areas busy throughout the weekend.

The Bicentennial flag is carried through the sky by a U.S. Army Golden Knights precision jumping team member during official dedication ceremonies at 12:00 noon on Saturday. The Golden Knights collected some beautiful memories of Cincinnati thanks to one brave jumper who carried a weighty camera attached to his helmet. The following day, a similar demonstration caused tense moments for spectators who witnessed a malfunction in a jumper's parachute. A safety chute was inflated, carrying the Golden Knight to a safe, and precise, landing.

See some familiar faces? In one of the year's most nostalgic moments, 88 of Cincinnati's greatest musicians, from today and years gone by, came together Sunday evening to sing "Celebrate '88" and to close The Dedication. The original song was written as the Commission's official event music. The audience was treated to individual performances by some of the participating groups before the finale, which was broadcast live by WCPO-TV9.

1. Thriftway Food • Drug Arches Overlook
2. Great American Broadcasting Company River Overlook
3. The Cincinnatus Statue
4. Quantum Chemical Corporation Heritage Garden
5. John Z. Herschede Summer Garden
6. Merrell Dow Pharmaceuticals River Overlook
7. Cincinnati Gateway Sculpture
8. The Kroger Company Promenade
9. Jack J. Smith Charitable Trust Access Ramps
10. Great Lawn
11. Procter & Gamble Performance Pavilion
12. The Cincinnati Gas & Electric Company River Overlook

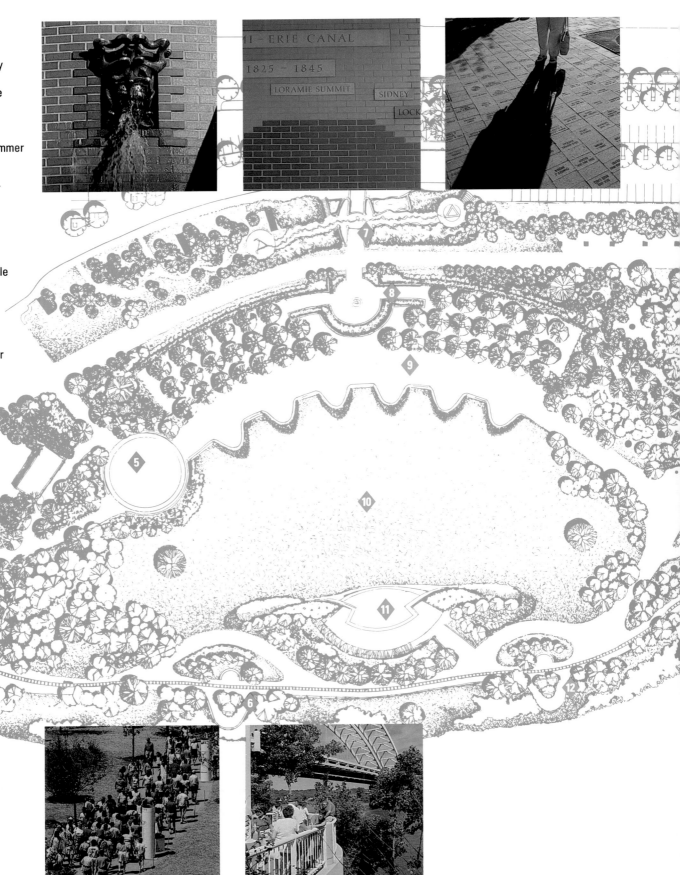

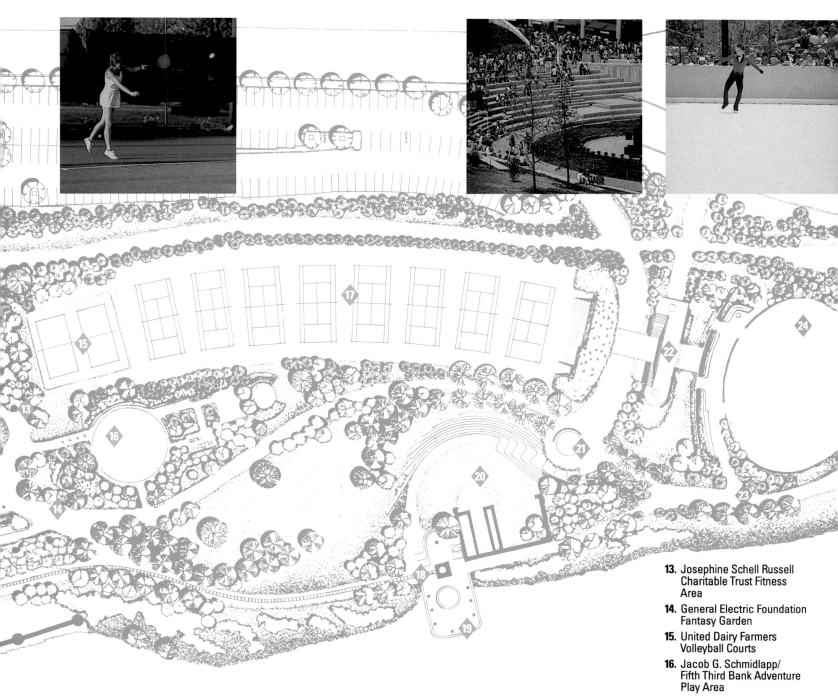

13. Josephine Schell Russell Charitable Trust Fitness Area

14. General Electric Foundation Fantasy Garden

15. United Dairy Farmers Volleyball Courts

16. Jacob G. Schmidlapp/ Fifth Third Bank Adventure Play Area

17. Carl H. Lindner Family Tennis Pavilion

18. Dr. Frederick A. Hauck Geological Timeline

19. Elijah Scott Fishing Pier

20. The Harold C. Schott Foundation Amphitheater

21. Robert H. Reakirt Foundation Amphitheater Overlook

22. Lazarus Skating Pavilion

23. Louise Taft Semple Foundation Winter Garden

24. The First National Bank of Cincinnati Skating Rink

THE HOMECOMING

In some ways, The Homecoming posed the greatest physical challenge to staff members, for it was actually five separate events packed within a ten-day period. It all began in 1984 when the Commission's Homecoming Committee put its sights on Riverfront Stadium as the location of the 1988 All-Star Game. Historically, the city was not in line to host this sports spectacular, but that fact hardly dampened the optimism of those planning the "grandest week in history." Positive thinking prevailed, and with the announcement of baseball's crown event scheduled here July 12th, the rest just fell into place.

The week began on July 3rd with a bigger-than-life parade. Gigantic fanciful floats, blue-ribbon marching bands, the thrill of the Bicentennial Herald Trumpets, historic regiments, vintage cars, colorful clowns and the grandiose regalia of a magnificent parade commanded the attention of 150,000 cheering spectators who braved the stifling combination of a 91° temperature and high humidity. 200 Years on Parade illustrated our city's history and its heritage through eight divisions, each depicting 25 years of achievement.

The Sports Greats Games, held during the first weeks of July, was actually a mini-Olympics which drew the participation of 2,800 young athletes and 5,000 spectators, coaches and volunteers. Winners in four age divisions, all 18 years and under, were treated with the surprise visit of a celebrity athlete who presented the trophies and other awards. Eleven sports comprised the Games, which were produced as a youthful prelude to the All-Star Game and a celebration of Cincinnati's rich sports heritage.

Other celebrities graced the city on Saturday, July 9th for Salute to Our Stars, a dazzling tribute to our hometown greats. These are the men and women whose contributions as artists, athletes, authors, doctors, entertainers, entrepreneurs, explorers, religious leaders, scientists and statesmen have earned them national, and in some cases international, acclaim. Easily, Roy Rogers was the hometown favorite. His easy-going way and infectious smile generated the greatest applause and most devoted following during his visit here. All the stars were introduced to a gathering of fans who lined a red carpet leading into the Convention Center, where a fabulous dinner and multi-media presentation highlighting each of the 53 honorees awaited Salute ticket-holders.

The next evening, the skies exploded in music, bright lights and colorful fireworks, fireworks, and more fireworks shot from the tops of downtown buildings. Lightbeams bisected the display, creating a heart-stopping panorama for an estimated 400,000 residents who began scouting viewing spots early in the afternoon. Gathering on surrounding hills, the crowds enjoyed an incredibly involved production of sight and sound as the "world's largest birthday cake" came to view through the magic of these giant, synchronized sparklers. Had they only known that in the first minutes of the performance a small fire had started on one of the participating building tops! It was, of course, quickly extinguished, but not before causing high blood pressure in more than a few Safety and Commission officials.

And the next day (one can almost feel the exhaustion setting in), bright and early, the Home of Professional Baseball exhibit was dedicated by none other than Baseball Commissioner Peter Ueberroth, just minutes before the All-Star Workout & Skills Competition was to begin. This computer-generated award-winning exhibit lines the covered Skywalk leading to Riverfront Stadium, calling out the "firsts" in Cincinnati baseball history.

Bicentennial Commission staff got a break the next day; the All-Star Game was not in its "jurisdiction." However, the city closed The Homecoming in grand style, with the pageantry of this most important American sporting event.

JULY 3 • 12, 1988

Each of the 8 divisions of 200 Years on Parade was lined up separately in the concrete parking areas lining Eggleston Avenue. Then the parade was pulled into place for its historic walk through downtown Cincinnati streets.

It was 91° according to the weatherman, but it seemed like the inside of an oven to parade participants, especially those dressed in authentic period clothing. Some had been waiting since early morning when their division was assembled.

At just a few minutes past 3:00 p.m. on July 3rd, The United States Marine Corps Band marched with sterling precision, creating a patriotic mood for this "Independence Day eve" event. Bicentennial officials purposely scheduled the Parade for July 3rd so as not to interfere with regularly scheduled July 4th community festivities.

This little boy had a front row seat to view the close to 90 units (some say it was exactly 88) in 200 Years on Parade.

The title banner for the grandest parade in Cincinnati's history proceeded the wrong way on Fifth Street. With the steep hills on both Broadway and Plum streets, the parade route had to be planned carefully. Neither people nor animals favor vertical angles! So, it was finally decided that Plum offered a smoother transition to Pete Rose Way, and therefore the Parade would march the wrong way on Fifth.

The Bicentennial Herald Trumpeters made their public debut during 200 Years on Parade. They absolutely thrilled spectators with their chilling rendition of the "Bicentennial Fanfare," written for this event.

2,000 square yards of blue carpet were pieced together and laid through the night, July 2nd, to add a "finishing touch" to the parade. The Bicentennial logo was hand-painted on the carpet, and positioned at the beginning of the route where WKRC-TV12 cameras televised the festivities live. Extending beyond the blue carpet was a blue line painted on either side of the street. Unfortunately, something happened during the mixing process and the blue line remains today on some sections of the parade route, despite repeated and industrial washings from City workers.

Even Abraham Lincoln came to wish Cincinnati Happy 200th Birthday! His carriage was one of many authentic historic carriages and automobiles on display during the 2½ hour parade.

Parade participants took extreme effort to assemble costumes and uniforms historically accurate, right down to the brass buttons.

From splashy bright red convertibles to vintage automobiles, the parade married past and present. But the older cars had a tough time battling the heat. One of the first to rumble down the route – a Crosley – died in the second block. A spectator and two staff members jumped up to give the car a push. It started, went about five feet, and then died again. So the gang rolled up their sleeves and began pushing again, but to no avail. Two blocks later the Crosley was laid to rest on the shady side of Sycamore Street.

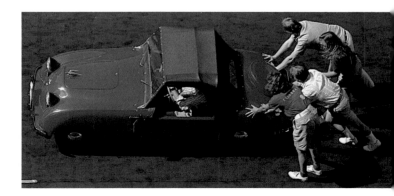

Fittingly, the final float was entitled "City of the Future," inspiring spectators to dream of what life will be like in Cincinnati's third century.

The Bicentennial Herald Trumpets sounded the start of a different kind of parade on July 9th. This procession was a glittering ensemble of Cincinnati's most beloved and respected sons and daughters whose contributions to fields from medicine to music have earned them national acclaim. Fans caught glimpses of their favorite stars as they were escorted across a red carpet and into the Convention Center, where a dazzling dinner dance was highlighted with a presentation of gifts to the 53 honorees. The festivities were broadcast live by WXIX-TV19.

In 1984, the Commission set its sites on securing the All-Star Game for Cincinnati's Bicentennial year. The fact that many other cities preceded Cincinnati in the right to host this crowning event did not deter representatives from the Commission, City and the Reds from scoring the winning home run!

Inside Riverfront Stadium, a record attendance of 55,837 fans watched the American League win the 59th annual Major League All-Star Game with a score of 2-1.

★   ★   ★

On their way to the Stadium, fans passed under the "Home of Professional Baseball" exhibit, honoring Cincinnati's baseball heritage.

Vehicular traffic coming into the downtown area was restricted beginning at 6:00 p.m. to allow ample time for positioning the mortars at the shooting sites – including the rooftops of five building towers – for the Bicentennial Fireworks. In repeated releases and extensive publicity issued from the Commission, residents were urged to find a viewing location on the surrounding hilltops. And beginning mid-afternoon, blankets and boomboxes began dotting the gentle slopes of our "seven" hills.

During the 10:00 p.m. Fireworks show, with music and memories courtesy of WLW and WEBN radio stations, 5,000 5-12″ shells and 2,500 Roman Candles were ignited to create a dazzling display of pyrotechnic genius. Those at home were treated to the spectacle thanks to WLW-TV5.

Just minutes into the spectacular show, Commission and Safety officials monitoring the shooting sites received the dreaded message on their radios: "We have a working fire." A shrub on the terraced-level of one of the five participating buildings had ignited. Within a few moments the blaze was extinguished, and heart rhythms and blood pressures dropped to a "high anxiety" level until the last shell had been fired.

TALL STACKS

Two very short words, yet they evoke such emotion, such wondrous memories. One million people came to Cincinnati's riverfront October 13-16th to celebrate Tall Stacks and a nostalgic return to the stern-wheeler age in America.

It was an event which had been in the planning stage for four years, one which had never been done before and, according to the riverboat captains, would not happen in Cincinnati in 1988. Tall Stacks posed monumental logistical concerns. Catering, concessions, river traffic, garbage removal, laundry service…all and more had to be coordinated on a minute-by-minute basis in the midst of hundreds of thousands of people navigating their way along Serpentine Wall and the Public Landing where the boats would be docked.

And then ticket-holders had to be guided to their appropriate vessel, and Passport holders had to find their way on as many riverboats as possible from 2:00 to 9:00 p.m. on Thursday and 7:00 to 10:00 a.m. the remaining days. On Saturday and Sunday, the unique challenges of synchronizing the frenzied flavor of a riverboat race kept the pace lively.

Not everything went as smoothly as planners had hoped. Up until the very last minute, problems were popping up and being resolved by a resourceful and dedicated group of nearly 4,000 volunteers and staff members. Looking back, the good far outweighed the bad.

The hills were bursting into the brilliant reds and golds of autumn. The sun shone brightly during three of the four days, and at night there was an abundance of twinkling stars and moonlight.

The riverfront was almost magically transformed into the "hustle and bustle" frenzy of the Port of Cincinnati 150 years before, thanks to costumed storytellers, brightly-colored exhibit modules relaying riverboat lore and an expansive facade of 1850's building fronts erected on the Public Landing. Truly, the mystique of the "Tom Sawyer" days was re-discovered on the banks of the Ohio River amidst the gathering of these beautiful American treasures.

Young and old came to experience the romance and wonder of an age gone by. In some cases, 70 years separated two hands holding tightly to one another, but the twinkle in their eyes was the very same. Tall Stacks was savored by all: the 56,000 who purchased cruise tickets, the 25,000 who had Passports, and the 919,000 others who came to see and to listen. Bicentennial Commons, Serpentine Wall and the Public Landing were packed with a constant moving flow of visitors enjoying not only the spectacle of the riverboats, but also a broad spectrum of entertainment. Multiple stages throughout the venue offered folk, bluegrass, dixieland, jazz, blues, cajun cookin', John Hartford and Glen Campbell.

It would be difficult to choose between the arrival and departure ceremonies as to which produced the greatest emotion. It was 4:00 p.m. on Friday, October 14th when the faint sounds of the calliope on board *The Steamboat Delta Queen* were first heard as she headed into port. Welcoming banners dropped from the Suspension Bridge as each of the 14 riverboats was introduced and met by a gathering of local dignitaries. From far down the river, residents had lined the shores to witness this historic parade.

And just 50 hours later, this distinguished gathering was preparing to leave, with honors presented to the captains, a bursting of fireworks, and "America the Beautiful" providing a musical backdrop. Again, the *Delta Queen* led the parade as handkerchiefs waved "good-bye" and more than a few tears dampened faces of all who had experienced these magnificent days.

Tall Stacks was the crowning glory of a sterling tribute to our past, present and future as the center of commerce in the Ohio Valley. It was a shining moment for all. Of course, it is impossible to please everyone. There was the young man who was quite upset to learn the Tall Stacks was not coming back in 1989!

P.S. The "oars are in motion" for a repeat performance in the next three to five years. Keep your cameras loaded!

OCTOBER 14 • 16, 1988

TALL STACKS
1788 CELEBRATE CINCINNATI 1988

P. A

The sanctuary of the Monastery in Mt. Adams was used to apply the 375 gallons of donated paint to the facade. It took a core group of three scenery painters more than 300 hours to produce this mid-1800's "main street" effect for Tall Stacks.

The *Southern Belle* from Chattanooga travelled the longest distance, 1,100 river miles, to come to Tall Stacks. The drought during the summer months caused some concern for those boats navigating rivers other than the Ohio, which is actually a series of pools controlled by dams. What did furrow the foreheads of some pilots were the six bridges, with staggered pier locations, within a 2-mile span at the Port of Cincinnati.

The first boat to arrive was The President on Monday evening. Her passage into the Port was followed in earnest by local television stations, and she was welcomed by a sizeable and appreciative crowd. The last boat to say "good-bye" was the Island Queen, who did not head for her home port of Memphis until Tuesday afternoon.

Passport tour lines were thousands strong by 7:30 a.m. Preparations for cruises caused some boats to close their Passport lines early, leaving guests to peek through the windows later in the day. Many of the 25,000 who purchased the souvenir booklet wanted only the colorful stamps designed for each boat. More stamping stations were opened to accommodate the demand, and even after the event, the Commission stamped Passports at its Reception Center in The Westin Atrium for several weeks.

Stretching down the Ohio, riverboat after riverboat followed *The Steamship Delta Queen* – the flagship of Tall Stacks – into their docking area during jubilant arrival ceremonies Friday afternoon. Captains were greeted by welcoming parties of local dignitaries who escorted them to the stage where they were treated to an enthusiastic audience of thousands gathered for that historic occasion.

At any given time, hundreds of thousands of smiling festival-goers lined the riverfront. When not watching the boats, an ever-changing kaleidoscope of performers kept toes tapping and hands clapping, all the way up to a rousing concert by country music great Glen Campbell on Sunday evening.

The network morning news shows sent their stars to Cincinnati during major events. CBS's "This Morning" weatherman Mark McEwen was live June 3rd from Bicentennial Commons. In the midst of Homecoming festivities, Joan Lundon and Charles Gibson of ABC's "Good Morning America" did their show on the riverfront. And October 14th, NBC's "Today Show" sent Willard Scott whose weather reports were serenaded by calliopes. On Sunday, Maria Shriver and Garrick Utley shared Tall Stacks with viewers of the "Sunday Today" show.

Before Tall Stacks, it was predicted one would be able to walk from shore to shore without ever touching the water. The prediction rang true. It has been estimated that 10,000 pleasure boats lined the riverfront from Coney Island to Ludlow, Kentucky. Within the Port of Cincinnati, pleasure boats and barge traffic were restricted to the southern one-third of the Ohio, an operational decision that kept activities running smoothly and safely.

The Tall Stacks captains were quite the heroes during their stay, posing for photographs and signing untold number of autographs. The captain of the *Belle of Louisville* finally resorted to carrying a stamp of his name to relieve his writer's cramp! This celebrity status has most assuredly helped in Cincinnati's efforts to bring the Tall Stacks back in the early 1990's.

Were it not for the modern clothing, one would have thought Tall Stacks had taken the city through a time machine, transporting all back to the mid-1800's and the hustle-and-bustle of the Port of Cincinnati. Riverboats clogged the Ohio riverfront. Bales of hay and barrels filled with various products lined the shores. Thanks to the authenticity achieved in the design of the storefront facade and the many props, an unforgettable ambiance filled the Public Landing.

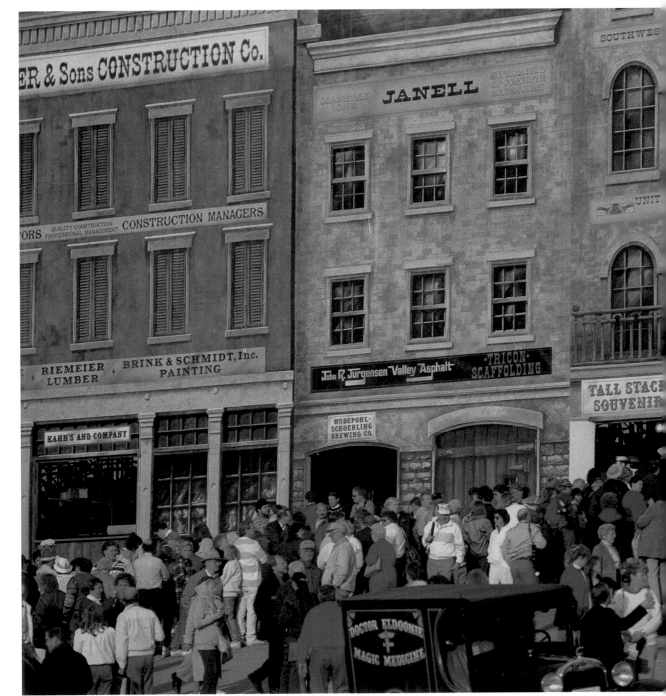

Saturday's 10-mile riverboat race between the *Mark Twain, Becky Thatcher, Southern Belle* and *River Queen* was a white-knuckled adventure as the riverboats juggled for first position. Cincinnati's own *Becky Thatcher* squeaked by to win the trophy, and the post-race captain's commentaries were filled with the spice of cheatin' and foolery that is the spirit of all great riverboat races.

The *Delta Queen* and *Belle of Louisville* gave their engine rooms quite a workout during Sunday's 2-mile race. The *Delta Queen's* captain was somewhat confused by Cincinnati's multiple bridges, and cut her engines one bridge early. When the *Belle* steamed ahead, the *Delta Queen* pushed with everything she had. Just a few seconds later, she literally inched by the *Belle* to a victorious finish.

"I think the most enjoyable of all races is a steamboat race...this is a sport that makes a body's very liver curl with enjoyment. A horse race is pretty tame and colorless in comparison."   Mark Twain

The Captain's Ball Friday evening honored the men and woman who made Tall Stacks a reality. To commemorate their participation in this historic event, each captain received a ship's bell engraved with an inscription denoting the boat's name, the event and its date. These beautiful bells now hang on the Tall Stacks as a constant reminder of this Cincinnati celebration of the stern-wheeler era.

Tall Stacks generated international publicity for Cincinnati, with reporters from England, Japan and Russia and all major news services in the U.S. filing stories on the pageantry celebrated that October weekend. In total, 350 reporters covered Bicentennial events in 1988, creating $17 million worth of publicity centered on Cincinnati.

A glowing fountain moored in the Ohio added a special gleam to the color of Tall Stacks.

Tears began to fall as a chorus of "America the Beautiful" filled the air during closing ceremonies Sunday. Then the moan of whistles blowing steam, lilting sounds of calliopes, colored sprays from fireboats and a splash of fireworks blended in a fast-paced farewell that ended a magnificent weekend all too quickly. It was beautiful, a perfect and precious memory for the 1 million people who shared the magic of Tall Stacks. WLW-TV5 telecast the departure ceremonies live to share the Tall Stacks farewell with the residents.

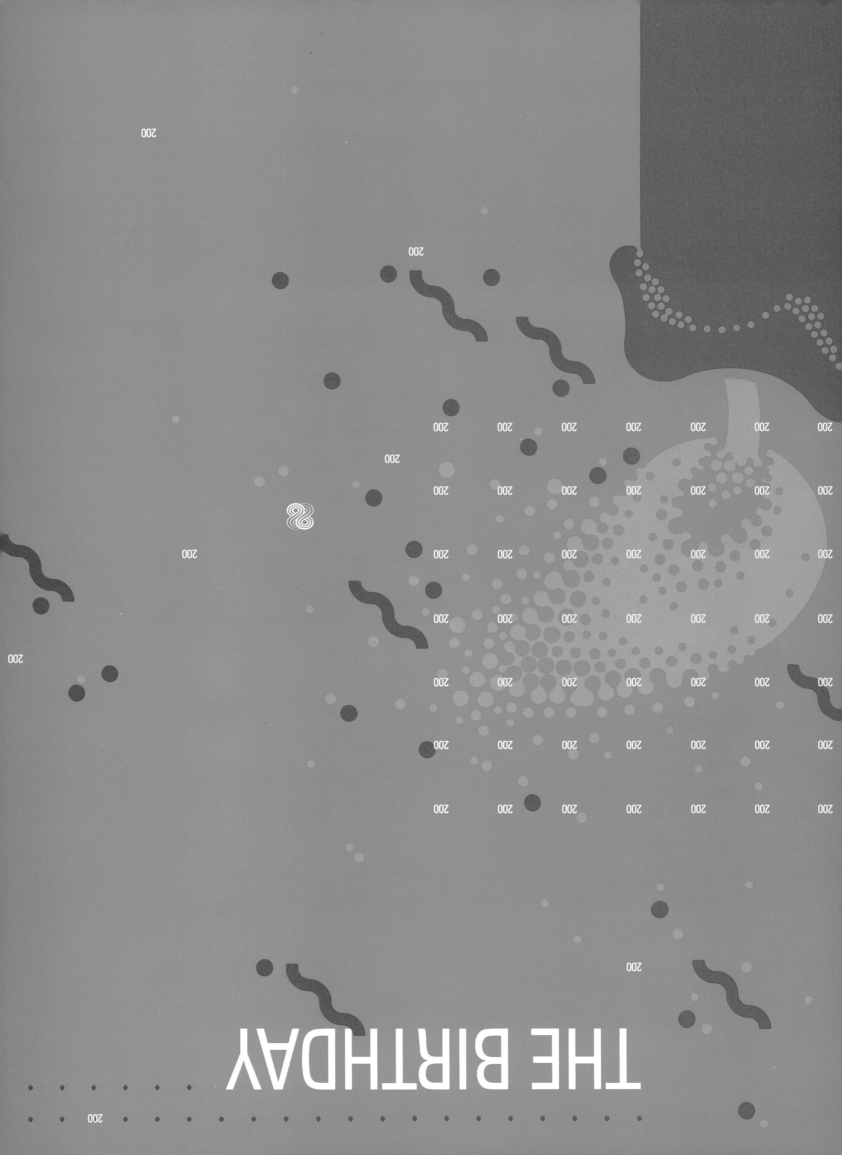

While some riverboats left directly after closing cere- monies, most made their quiet departure during the early morning fog.

The banjo-picking tune "Tall Stacks Are Comin' Back to Town" was written and performed by riverboat pilot and musician John Hartford in celebration of Cincinnati's salute to the stern-wheeler age. Hartford performed the song during arrival ceremonies as the boats navigated their way into port.

Weather wise, the year ended in as nasty manner as it had begun. December 28th, Cincinnati's actual 200th birthday, dawned without benefit of inviting sunshine. Instead, snow and ice carpeted the streets and highways, and bitter cold temperatures mixed with seemingly gale-force winds kept all but the bravest souls in the warmth of their homes.

At 9:30 a.m. it was decided by Commission staff that the re-enactment of the first landing scheduled to take place at the river's edge at the Public Landing would be moved to the security of the Convention Center. It was a tough decision, for this play, complete with an authentic flatboat pulling up to shore and settlers disembarking, was wonderfully scripted, acted and designed. And the natural ambiance created by standing at the exact spot our forefathers came to shore 200 years ago was all but lost within the Convention Center's doors.

The 400 descendants of the founding families who were gathered for an awards and scroll-signing ceremony prior to the re-enactment were disappointed that the play had been moved indoors. They were bundled appropriately in layers of wool, ready to brave the elements as their forefathers had done.

But the Public Landing was laden with ice, the river was rising rapidly, its current strong, and the wind force at the water's edge was unbearable.

By 12:00 noon when the festivities began at the Convention Center for this final Bicentennial event, the sun had begun to peek through the clouds, the snow flurries were long gone and the ice was melting from the streets. But Cincinnatians have this thing about snowy weather.... So instead of having perhaps 30,000 people in attendance – it was a school holiday – there were approximately 15,000 who came to wish Cincinnati an official "Happy Birthday," make a wish for its third century and eat a piece of birthday cake and ice cream.

A sampling of the year's best entertainment was on hand throughout the day. A silent auction of Bicentennial memorabilia – from banners to bugles – was a hot spot for bargain hunters. And area students displayed the contents of time capsules they created, a treasury of thoughts and things to puzzle and delight youngsters in the year 2088.

Toward the evening, the crowd began to thicken in anticipation of the opening of the Centennial Time Capsule, which was extracted from City Hall several weeks before. On live television, a Brinks armored truck drove into the Convention Center to deliver a piece of Cincinnati history. The drama increased as the capsule's seals were broken, and the contents revealed. Letters, documents, a Cincinnati Police manual...nothing quite as imaginative as what the students had collected, but of great interest and significance to local historians.

The Bicentennial Birthday ended in a most appropriate way: a video capturing the emotions of the year's greatest moments, a huge flickering cake wheeled in by volunteers, and a resounding rendition of "Happy Birthday." Tears glistened in the eyes of Commission staff members gathered there at that moment. It was over. Finally. Unbelievably. Hopefully, their feelings were shared by those gathered in the Convention Center, and those watching the finale on television in their homes. It was a grand year. Perhaps our very best.

DECEMBER 28, 1988

200

The December 27th dress re-hearsal for the re-enactment of the landing of first settlers went perfectly, holding promise for a memorable performance. The flatboat had a bit of trouble crossing the Ohio, but the fol-lowing day it would be coming downstream only a few hundred feet, so it was of no concern. However, December 28th dawned with freezing rain and snow. By 9:30 a.m., safety for performers and the audience led Commission officials to move the re-enactment to the Convention Center to begin the Birthday festivities at 12:00 noon.

Authenticity was a goal of re-enactment planners, right down to the costumes and script. The audience, including 400 descendants of the original settlers, saw as close a representation as history books allow as to what occurred during the hours after the first families landed at Yeatman's Cove.

The December 27th Bicentennial Ball was an evening gala of fantasy and frills to honor all Bicentennial volunteers and contributors.

Descendants of the founding families, some coming from as far away as California, were honored at an early morning reception during which they each signed a special scroll which will be preserved in the Bicentennial Time Capsule. The founding families' scroll was ceremoniously presented to one of the youngest descendants during the re-enactment play, signalling the passage of 200 years and the promise of our third century.

Birthday cake and ice cream for all – isn't that the foundation of birthday parties? The tiered cake glowing with tapers was ceremoniously cut by one of Cincinnati's most respected and beloved citizens, Frederick A. "Fritz" Hauck, who shares the city's birthday. A large crowd sang "Happy Birthday" to Cincinnati and then the scrumptious treats were distributed free throughout the day.

The 15,000 people who attended The Bicentennial Birthday got a chance to leave their mark on history by signing an electronic scroll which is included in the Bicentennial Time Capsule.

The excitement surrounding
the live television coverage of
the opening of the Centennial
Time Capsule was heightened
by the arrival of a Brink's truck
carrying the sealed capsule.
Weeks before it had been removed from a cornerstone at
City Hall. Its contents were revealed in front of thousands in
the Convention Center, and
many more watching from
home.

Local celebrities and noted historians were on hand to examine and share the message left us from our forefathers 100 years ago. A police department manual, December 28, 1888 newspaper, City Hall and Board of Education directories and several coins were among the contents. To return the favor, a Bicentennial Time Capsule will present a peak into life in the 20th century. Inclusive of this publication and the 2 Birthday scrolls, the capsule harbors a diverse collection of fact and fad, and a special birthday wish for tricentennial celebrants.

Cincinnatus led the parade of a "made for television" cake to signal the final minutes of the WLW-TV5 program and the Bicentennial year. The Herald Trumpets gave their last performance and Commission Chairman Joseph S. Stern, Jr. and Mayor Charles Luken recalled the magnificent memories the year had produced. Balloons fell from above, cascading down upon a cheering crowd. And so the Bicentennial year ended, with a moving combination of smiles and tears.

PROGRAMS

To showcase the richness of Cincinnati's heritage, an impressive array of arts, education and community programs was designed by nearly 500 citizens working on Bicentennial committees. This blending of talents resulted in a year filled with activities which involved every age group and interest.

When the Commission was founded, one of its primary goals was to celebrate Cincinnati's rich cultural heritage in a way that would involve all citizens. That translated into planning a series of smaller events, or programs, which would invite residents to be a part of the planning process or to be entertained by the outcome!

One of the most immediate concerns was to develop new curriculum materials for local school systems whose outdated history lessons could not ignite the imaginations of young minds. And it was those young minds that should understand the significance of the city's 200th year. The Commission worked in earnest with education and history professionals who dedicated themselves to enlightening area schoolchildren, and their families, about the tapestry of people and events which comprise Cincinnati's past and will shape its future.

The bountiful response to this need resulted in the publication of excellent activities guides and textbooks, and a high level of student participation in a variety of projects all of which shared the Bicentennial experience with our future leaders.

In studying Cincinnati's history, one of the strongest threads woven through the years is our love and support of the arts. It was critical that this vital and energetic passion of our past and present be personified in a collection of programs dedicated to theater, music, painting and other artistic endeavors. Therefore, much time and effort was directed to the production of a series of exhibits and performances that called upon local artisans to share their tremendous talents.

The ideas flowed endlessly. And when the fund-raising campaign was completed, the most difficult task facing the Commission was deleting the arts programs which had not received financial support. Still, the mixture of the arts which filled 1988 is memorable and remarkable.

Close to $1 million in contributions by area businesses and individuals was collected to fund the myriad of Bicentennial programs. Some were tailored to specific interests and audiences, while others embrace the entire community. Collectively, they spoke to an important facet of our lives, an important time in our history. And each person who took advantage of this year-round exploration of our heritage has a deeper feeling for Cincinnati.

SEPTEMBER, 1986 · DECEMBER, 1988

"Step into History" was the campaign theme for personalized bricks to be placed in Bicentennial Commons, Covington's Riverside Drive and Newport's Taylor Park. Walkways in these 3 locations immortalize the names of 35,000 people whose purchase of a Bicentennial Brick helped fund other celebration activities.

A comprehensive visual identity program of colors, patterns and typography was designed for the bicentennial celebration. This festive "look" was applied to all official publications, merchandise, environmental design and signage to present a consistent theme in the design of all facets of the celebration.

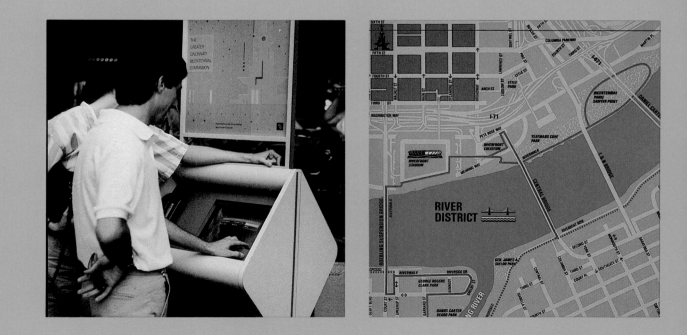

HOME OF PROFESSIONAL BASEBALL EXHIBIT

July 11, 1988

Commission Executive Director Richard Greiwe, Reds Owner Marge Schott, Baseball Commissioner Peter Ueberroth and Commission Chairman Joseph S. Stern, Jr. were on hand to dedicate this tribute to Cincinnati's baseball heritage. Beginning with the Red Stockings and ending with Pete Rose's historic "4192", the exhibit calls out the "firsts" in Cincinnati baseball history and lines the covered Skywalk leading to Riverfront Stadium.

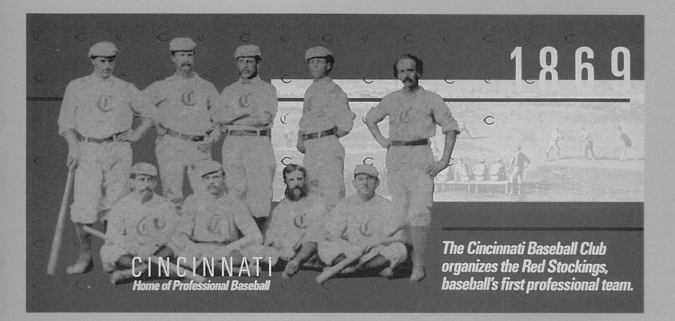

1869

CINCINNATI
Home of Professional Baseball

The Cincinnati Baseball Club organizes the Red Stockings, baseball's first professional team.

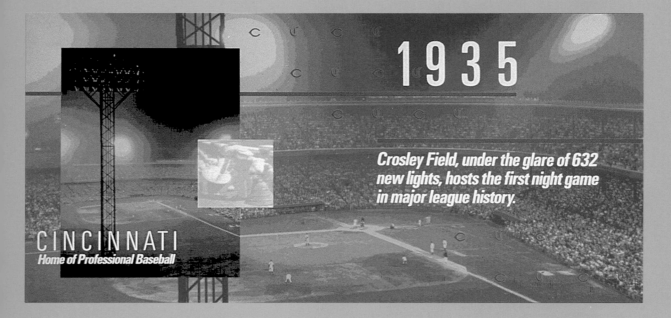

1935

CINCINNATI
Home of Professional Baseball

Crosley Field, under the glare of 632 new lights, hosts the first night game in major league history.

COMMUNITY PANELS

January, 1987 - December, 1988
In 62 communities throughout the region, the history and heritage of that particular neighborhood, city, township or village are displayed on an outdoor panel installed in a central gathering place. The colorful map, anecdotes and "fun facts" illustrated on each side of the panel were collected from residents of that area. During 1988, the 62 panels travelled together to malls and other public locations to allow all residents to get to know each other, and learn about the character and personality of these Greater Cincinnati communities.

200 GREATER CINCINNATIANS

July 1, 1988

"The most memorable thing I remember about the Bicentennial is seeing the gleam in my 10-year-old son Kenny's eyes and his beaming smile as he waved a small American flag while his mother, chosen as one of the 200 Greater Cincinnatians, marched by in the Homecoming Parade." Those words from a proud father and husband signify the emotion and importance of this program. Two hundred residents of Greater Cincinnati were nominated by neighbors and friends who had witnessed their good deeds to fellow citizens in need. Each was presented a special Bicentennial medal during ceremonies July 1st, and two days later they were introduced to the public during the Parade. This program highlighted the strength of our community – its caring people.

P R O G R A M S

A R T S

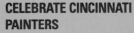

CELEBRATE CINCINNATI PAINTERS

August 31 - October 18, 1987
Regional painters brought forth an exceptional display of artistic impressions of our 200th birthday at this exhibition at The Art Academy of Cincinnati. Traditional and contemporary categories captured the city's spirit in two very different ways. The exhibition of these works was well-attended, and sent forth a strong message that the arts are alive and well in the impressive talents of artists who choose Greater Cincinnati as their home.

BICENTENNIAL CINCINNATI: THE CITY IN PHOTOGRAPHS

September 11 - December 26, 1987
A beautiful menagerie of secret places was captured by amateur and professional photographers who took to the city streets to immortalize a moment in time. A fresh look at an old building. A startling revelation of a place passed each day. In crisp black/white and spectacular color, the photographs produced from this competition were enjoyed by all who studied the fruits of the artists' labor which were on display at Images Gallery.

FROM FLATBOAT TO TOWBOAT: OHIO RIVER TRADITION
Fall, 1986

Almost as a prelude to Tall Stacks, this video documentary traced the traditions of work, storytelling and river personalities from the days of flatboats to the present diesel towboats. Winner of the coveted Golden Eagle Award from CINE, the video also featured interviews with river veterans now in their 70s and 80s, presenting an intriguing look at life on one of America's great waterways.

DR. MARTIN LUTHER KING, JR.: A TRIBUTE CONCERT
January 15 - 17, 1988

In commemoration of one of America's most influential civil rights leaders, the School for Creative and Performing Arts presented this original theatrical production. The musical was uplifting and memorable, according to audiences which enjoyed the performances and its broadcast on public television.

BICENTENNIAL QUILT
January - December, 1988

Vivid blues, greens, reds and yellows are blended together in a kaleidoscope of fabric which tells the story of our 200-year history. This fascinating patchwork of our past and present was bound by the single stitches of 8,804 Greater Cincinnati residents who visited the quilt as it traveled throughout the area. The finished artwork was unveiled on June 30, 1988, and is presently awaiting a permanent home where it will be shared with generations to come.

SAENGERFEST
May 1, 1988
The tradition of the German choral festival came to life in Music Hall through a harmonious collection of the region's most melodious choral groups. The original Saengerfests, dating to the mid-1800's, were gatherings of German singing societies and, in fact, their popularity in early Cincinnati led to the construction of Music Hall. Our Bicentennial year brought back this piece of our heritage, with complementing festivities in Washington Park and Findlay Market.

AUSTRALIA BICENTENARY EXCHANGE
Through 1988
Sydney, Australia became Cincinnati's sister city during 1988 in celebration of their mutual 200th birthdays. An Aboriginal art exhibit, film festival, folk music concert, international business meeting, social studies workshop and even a visit from "Tully" the koala gave Cincinnati an Australian flair throughout the year.

COLLAGE OF ARTS/FROM OUR PERSPECTIVE

May 17, 1988

Inspirational is a word that comes to mind when describing this wonderful artistic translation of memories shared by senior citizens. A batik artist, choreographer/dancer, painter and playwright interviewed elder residents from four area neighborhoods and, from their stories, created a stunning and heartwarming collage of art presented at Senior Expo.

A FRONTIER TALE

July 15 - August 14, 1988

The charm of the old traveling medicine show was revitalized in this enjoyable musical revue which starred a "flim-flam" man named Black Jack. When his energetic sales pitch for a magical elixir did not hold the attention of curious onlookers, Black Jack began to unravel a tale about the people he had met in his travels through the "heart of the land." His yarns entertained audiences in cities and towns within a 100-mile radius of Cincinnati.

ON THE BANKS

July 23, 27, and 29, 1988

Through the eyes and ears of two young children, audiences were introduced to several prominent figures from our past – including John Symmes, Dr. Daniel Drake, Harriet Beecher Stowe – in this newly-commissioned production. Ten original musical pieces punctuated this dramatic story of the people and principles which have shaped our past.

RIVER CROSSINGS
September 25, 1988
What it means to be black in Greater Cincinnati was passionately portrayed in this authentically-documented epic musical drama presented at Music Hall. Spanning two centuries, this original production shared important and meaningful reflections of the black community on our city's settlement and growth. Through song, dance and drama, the play ventured to fill some of the missing pieces in the overall history of our region.

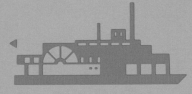

EDUCATION

BICENTENNIAL IMAGES
Throughout 1988
Thirty seconds of colorful commentary and visuals presented a slice of Cincinnati's life in 150 television spots aired on local stations during the year. These video vignettes presented our communities, landmarks and people in a new and different light, and increased awareness of our 200th birthday.

PORTRAITS IN EXCELLENCE
January - December, 1988
Premiering on Martin Luther King, Jr. Day, this stunning traveling exhibit celebrated 100 contemporary Greater Cincinnati black leaders, presenting an informative accounting of their contributions to our community and their impact on our future.

STORYTELLERS
Throughout 1988
The universal wish to go back
in time was fulfilled during 1988
through 12 local actors who
portrayed men and women
whose lives shaped our city's
development. Simon Kenton.
George Washington Williams.
Captain Mary Greene. Murray
Seasongood. Jennie D. Porter.
These and more came to life
through energetic performances which drew thousands
to listen and to learn. The
performances were also
broadcast on WCET-TV48.

ACTIVITIES BOOKLETS
Fall, 1987
From here came the answers to teachers' fervent prayers. Inside this simple-looking booklet were 101 ways to keep energetic minds and hands very busy. Elementary and junior/senior level teachers were offered – free of charge – this collection of innovative ideas designed to invite schoolchildren to be participants in the education of history. Hopefully, their use spread the word and the importance of our 200th birthday to these young students.

URBAN HISTORY SOURCEBOOKS
February, 1988
The name may sound rather cumbersome, but the contents of these sourcebooks are illuminating the minds of 4th/5th and 7th/8th graders throughout Cincinnati. They are filled with chapters on the people, places and events which influenced our past. With photographs, diary inserts, business ledgers and other innovative materials, this history publication received high marks from educators and students.

THE PRIDE AND THE PROMISE
October, 1987
Inspired by the spectacular Airport mosaics, this stunning publication captures the essence of our industrial development with a sparkling collection of quotes, anecdotes, and "fun facts." The book has a captivating story to tell of Cincinnati's evolution as the Queen City of the West, and offers a treasury of photographs and stories which highlight a vibrant period in our history.

BICENTENNIAL MASCOT
Throughout 1988
Students in nearly 350 area elementary schools became loyal fans and friends of Cincinnatus, the Bicentennial mascot. The fun-loving Cincinnatus visited schoolchildren during the first five months of the year to star in an original play written to teach students how the city was named. Then these young historians shared the story with their families and, soon, all of Cincinnati came to know of its namesake. This was an incredibly successful program with far-reaching public relations benefits for the Commission.

ESSAY CONTEST
April 21, 1988

"If experience is the best teacher, what experience over the past 200 years has prepared Cincinnati to face its future?" posed a challenging question to 10th through 12th graders who participated in this literary contest. For judges, the essays presented an enlightening view of our city's past achievements and future aspirations as seen through the eyes of its youth.

THE BICENTENNIAL GUIDE TO GREATER CINCINNATI: A PORTRAIT OF 200 YEARS
December, 1988

In 1943, a book on Cincinnati's economic, cultural and community development was published as a WPA project. The manual became an important resource to researchers, writers and historians. This 1988 update provides a wealth of information for everyone interested in our city's life.

SPORTS GREATS GAMES
July, 1988
This mini-Olympics drew the participation of 2,800 young athletes and 5,000 spectators, coaches and volunteers. Winners in four age divisions, all 18 years and under, were treated with the surprise visit of a celebrity athlete who presented the trophies and other awards. Eleven sports comprised the Games, which were produced as a youthful prelude to the All-Star Game and a celebration of Cincinnati's rich sports heritage.

RIVERWALK DEDICATION/ RIVER HISTORY RELAY

October 1, 1988

The historic stations along the Riverwalk presented a formidable test for hundreds of middle-school students who gathered in the early morning light for this relay of the minds. Teams were faced with a field of questions relating to each station along the way – railroads, river travel, bridge construction. The Relay ended with the "world's longest ribbon-cutting ceremony" to officially dedicate the Riverwalk. The ceremony was carried live by WKRC radio.

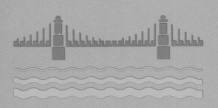

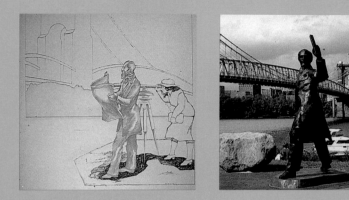

BOY SCOUT PLAZA DEDICATION
October 29, 1988
3,300 Boy Scouts marched from Fountain Square to Daniel Carter Beard's boyhood home in Covington to inaugurate dedication ceremonies for the Boy Scout Plaza. The Plaza pays tribute to Beard, the founder of the Boy Scouts.

BICENTENNIAL TIME CAPSULES

December 28, 1988

Maybe they will only stay sealed until our 250th anniversary, but time capsules created by area schoolchildren drew much attention during The Bicentennial Birthday. During the fall, students collected impressions of present day fashions and fads and "sealed" them in very creative containers. They began arriving in the Commission office in late December, and judges had a hard time selecting the winning entries from this student menagerie of life. The finalists were on display at the Birthday festivities, and their contents evoked a mixture of chuckles and concern from passers-by!

BLACK CINCINNATI: JOURNEY ACROSS TIME

December 26 - 27, 1988

At a time when historians from throughout the United States gathered in Cincinnati for an annual conference, an anthology of papers presented by four noted historians documented the black experience in Greater Cincinnati's history.

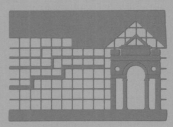

The Riverwalk is a four-mile heritage trail connecting the riverfronts of Cincinnati, Covington and Newport. From the dinosaurs that roamed this valley, to the area's early settlement and tremendous growth, to historical personalities, the Riverwalk illustrates our strong ties with the river.

Clearly marked by colorful tile pavement markers and signage, the walkway features thirty-six stations that tell a captivating story of Greater Cincinnati as the pivotal center of the Ohio River.

1. Flood Column
2. Cincinnati Arch
3. Tall Stacks
4. Canal Lock
5. Miami Erie Canal
6. Seven Hills
7. Canal Cut
8. Center Arch
9. Indian Masks
10. Serpent Steps
11. River Source
12. River Navigation
13. Ohio River
14. Bridges
15. Queen City
16. Fish Heads
17. River Mouth
18. Porkopolis
19. Fish of the Ohio River
20. Geologic Timeline
21. Cincinnatus Sculpture
22. Steamboats: A Way of Life
23. Early Cincinnati
24. Bridging the Ohio
25. Flatboat to Towboat
26. The Ohio: A Changing River
27. John A. Roebling
28. Simon Kenton
29. Mary Greene
30. James Bradley
31. Little Turtle
32. John J. Audubon
33. Daniel Carter Beard
34. Defending the Valley
35. Floods & Flood Walls
36. Changing Skyline

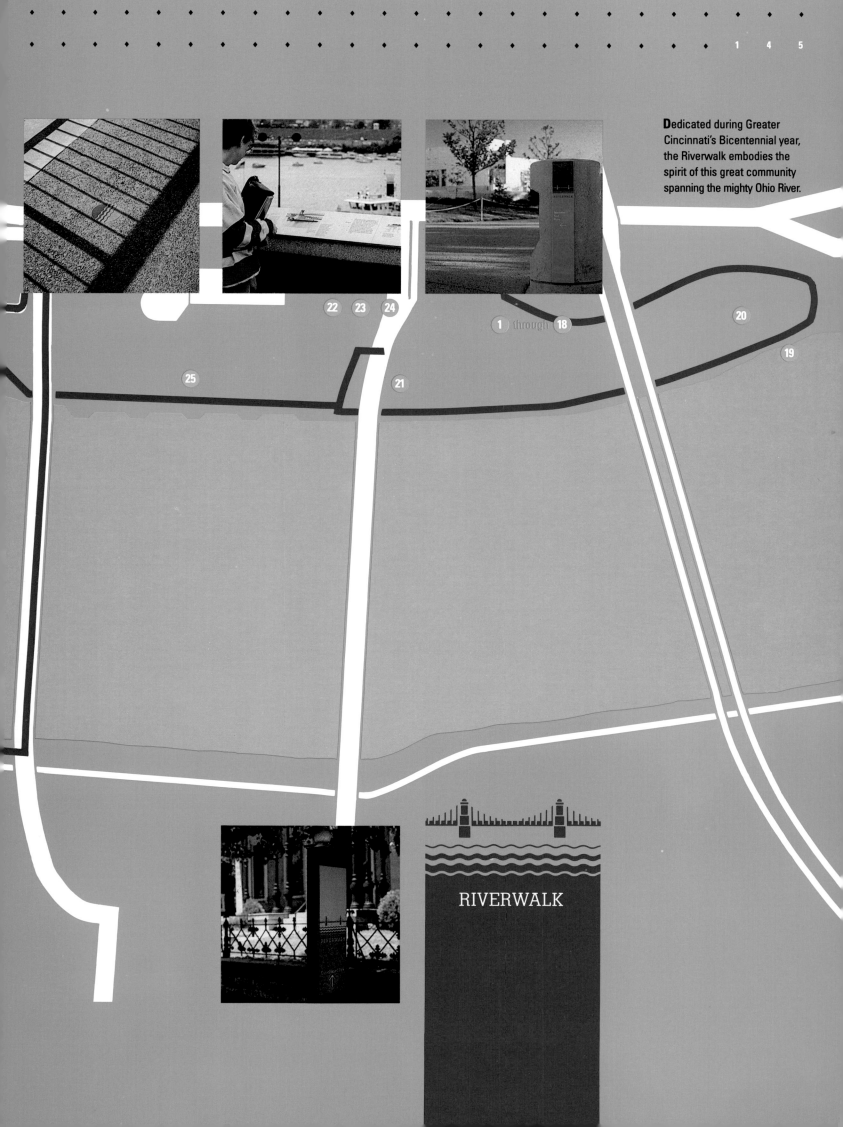

Dedicated during Greater Cincinnati's Bicentennial year, the Riverwalk embodies the spirit of this great community spanning the mighty Ohio River.

RIVERWALK

Hardly a week went by without some community activity scheduled to salute Cincinnati's bicentennial. This calendar presents a look back at a year filled with a myriad of special events created by local organizations and institutions to say "Happy 200th Birthday".

J A N U A R Y

Dec. 31	The Countdown
through Jan. 3	"An American Painter Abroad: Frank Duveneck's European Years" at Art Museum
through Feb. 28	"Prints & Drawings by Frank Duveneck & His Circle" at Art Museum
through Jan. 10	"Cincinnati Collects Christmas" at Taft Museum
through Jan. 3	Holiday Skies at Planetarium
through Jan. 3	Winterfest at Kings Island
through Jan. 3	Festival of Lights at Cincinnati Zoo
through Feb. 6	"Wildlife in Art" at Museum of Natural History
through Dec. 28	Masonic Temple Tours
2, 3	The Boar's Head & Yule Log Festival at Christ Church
6-20	Community Panels Traveling Exhibit at Eastgate Mall
10	Cincinnati Chamber Orchestra Concert at Old St. Mary's
12-Feb. 7	"Clear Liquor & Coal Black Nights" at Playhouse in the Park
15-17	"A Celebration of Brotherhood Through Music – Tribute to Martin Luther King, Jr." at School for Creative & Performing Arts
18	"Portraits in Excellence" at Convention Center
22, 23	"Forgotten Crossroads" by Cincinnati Folk Life at Art Museum
28-Mar. 10	Australian Aboriginal Arts Exhibit at Cincinnati Public Library

F E B R U A R Y

4-Mar. 20	"Nicholas Longworth–Art Patron of Cincinnati" at Taft Museum
6	"The Cotton Club" at Convention Center
10-23	Community Panels Traveling Exhibit at Swifton Commons
13-May 1	"Duncanson and Longworth: The Artist and His Patron" at Art Museum
22-27	Bicentennial Quilt on Display at Bonham Library
25-Mar. 9	Community Panels Traveling Exhibit at Beechmont Mall
29-Mar. 27	"U.S.S.R. Individual, Family, Society" Exhibit at Union Terminal
29-Mar. 5	Bicentennial Quilt on Display at West Fork Library
Feb., Mar., April	Jazz-Live from the Hyatt

M A R C H

3	Hannaford Dialogue Series at College Hill Town Hall
3-6	Appalachian Fling at Eastgate Mall
4-Apr. 1	"Cincinnati: Yesterday and Today" Exhibit at Tangeman Fine Arts Gallery
11-May 7	Jim Dine Exhibit at Contemporary Arts Center
13	Marsh Series Delphin and Romain, Piano Duo at Art Museum
15-22	Community Panels Traveling Exhibit at Tri-County Mall
18-Apr. 2	Spiral Festival at Turfway Park Race Course
20	American Negro Spiritual Festival at Music Hall
21-26	Bicentennial Quilt on Display at Anderson Branch Library
24-Apr. 5	Community Panels Traveling Exhibit at Northgate Mall
25	Yearlings Historic Home Tour Fine Antiques and Artwork in Burlington, KY
27	Marsh Series Carolyn Sebron, Solo Recital at Art Museum
28-Apr. 4	Bicentennial Quilt on Display at Cincinnati Public Library

A P R I L

1-June	West End Historical Tour at Taft High School
1-Oct. 28	Bicentennial Reception Center Open at The Westin Atrium
2	The Jim Beam Stakes at Turfway Park
2	The Flying Cloud Academy of Vintage Dance 1888 Cincinnati Centennial Exposition Ball at University YMCA
4	Findlay Market Parade - Downtown
4	Reds' Opening Day at Riverfront Stadium
4-30	Bicentennial Quilt Stitching at Norwood Library, CG&E, Twin Towers Retirement Community and Glenway Dodge
9-May 30	Brighten Up Cincinnati '88 Spring Clean Up Programs
10	UC/Over-The-Rhine Planning & Historic Perspectives Discussion at Steuben Hall/UC
10	Marsh Series David Baker/Larry Ridley/Joe Kennedy, Jr. Quintet with Keith Copeland & Russell Wilson at Art Museum
10-June	"The Framework of the Frontier: Early Cinti. Architecture & the Baum-Taft House" at Taft Museum

13-19	Community Panels Traveling Exhibit at Cincinnati Zoo
15-17	The Ohio Genealogical Society Seminar at Kings Island Inn
17	Lung Association Bicentennial Walk at Yeatman's Cove
18	Senior Olympics at Fountain Square
21	Bicentennial Essay Contest Awards Ceremony at Mercantile Library
21-May 3	Community Panels Traveling Exhibit at Florence Mall
23	"Duncanson and Longworth: The Artist and His Patron" Symposium at Art Museum
23	Jazz to End Hunger at Riverfront Coliseum
27	Australian World Trade Assoc. Dinner at Omni Netherland Plaza
28	Charles P. Taft Memorial Lecture at Christ Church
29	Cincinnati Children's Theatre's Bicentennial Musical at Taft Theatre
30	"Harvard Comes to the Ohio Valley" at Westin Hotel Cincinnati
29-30	Women's Theatre of Cinti. Presents "Wild Cincinnati Women Don't Get the Blues" at Gabriel's Corner
30	Friends of Amistad: "History of & Tribute to Black Organizations in Cincinnati" at Carrousel Inn

M A Y

May-Dec. 88	"Judaica Heirlooms: A Bicentennial Sampler" Exhibit at Hebrew Union College
1	Saengerfest '88 at Music Hall
2-30	Bicentennial Quilt Stitching at Northgate Mall, Marquardt House, Wullenweber Motors, and Taft Museum
3-Sept. 4	"Simply Stunning: 200 Years of Fashion in America" at Art Museum
6-8	Women's Theatre of Cinti. Presents "Wild Cincinnati Women Don't Get the Blues" at Gabriel's Corner
6-12	Australian Film Festival at Kenwood Cinemas
8	Clifton Tour of Historical Houses
10	Dedication of Cincinnatus Statue at Bicentennial Commons
12-15	Alexander Zemlinsky's "The Chalk Circle" at Corbett Auditorium/UC
13, 14, 20-22	Southern Gateway Chorus Salute to the Bicentennial at College of Mt. St. Joseph
13-15	Appalachian Festival at Coney Island

15	"Faith, Farms, and Fatback: A Culture Preserved" Slide Presentation at Steuben Hall/UC
15	Jewish Folk Festival at Burnet Woods Bandshell
16-22	Mazda LPGA Championship at Jack Nicklaus Sports Center
18	Bicentennial Lecture by Dr. Kammen, Pulitzer Prize Winning Historian at Tangeman University Center/UC
19-30	Community Panels Traveling Exhibit at Western Woods Mall
20-22	Maifest '88 at MainStrasse
20-22, 27, 28	May Festival at Music Hall
21	Afro-American Heritage Day at Fountain Square
21	Mason-Dixon Steeplechase
21	Cincinnati Park Board "Green Up Day"
27-29	Hotfest '88 at Convention Center
28-30	Balloonfest '88 at Coney Island
29	Westennial at Dunham Recreation Complex
29-30	Taste of Cincinnati - Downtown
30	Cincinnati Youth Symphony Orchestra Bicentennial Concert at Eden Park

J U N E

3-12	The Dedication at Bicentennial Commons
3-July 10	Tully, The Koala, Returns at Cincinnati Zoo
4	Kid's Fest
4-5	Oscar Robertson Tennis Tournament at Bicentennial Commons
4	Kings Men Chorus "Salute to Cincinnati" at Memorial Hall
9-12	Panegyri Greek Festival at Greek Orthodox Church
10-11	Cincinnati Regatta & Olympic Rowing Trials at East Fork State Park
11	Bicentennial Square Dance Celebration at Yeatman's Cove
12	Cincinnati Bicentennial Jazzfest at Bicentennial Commons
12	German Day Festival at Strickers Grove
17-19	Delta Kings Barbershop Chorus "School Daze" at Princeton High School
17-19	Summerfair '88 at Coney Island
18-Nov. 20	"The Starwatchers"–Cincinnati Skies at Planetarium

24-26	Taste of Northern Kentucky at MainStrasse
25	"Search Cincinnati" Greater Cincinnati Council of Camp Fire, Inc. at Fountain Square
30	Cincinnati Opera's "Susannah" at Music Hall

J U L Y

1	200 Greater Cincinnatians Awards Presentation at Bicentennial Commons
1	Bicentennial Quilt on Display at Westin Atrium
2	Cincinnati Opera Presents "Susannah" at Music Hall
2-10	Sports Greats Games
3-12	The Homecoming
3	200 Years on Parade - Downtown
3	125th Anniversary of the First Baptist Church
4	WUBE All-American Birthday Party: Bicentennial Edition at Bicentennial Commons
4	Pleasant Run Farms Bicentennial Parade
5-24	"Tintypes" Musical at Showboat Majestic
5-30	Cincinnati Union Terminal Mosaic Studies at Michael Lowe Gallery
5-Dec. 28	Cincinnati Masonic Temple Tours: "Step Back into History"
8-Aug. 27	"Diamonds Are Forever" Exhibition at Contemporary Arts Center
9	Salute to Our Stars at Convention Center
9	Stephen Foster Festival at Alms Park
9-13	The Cincinnati Classic at Music Hall
10	Skyline Bicentennial Fireworks - Downtown
10	Equitable Old Timers Game at Riverfront Stadium
11	All-Star Skills Competition & Workout at Riverfront Stadium
12	All-Star Game at Riverfront Stadium
15-Sept. 15	Golden Monkey Exhibit at Cincinnati Zoo
15-31	"A Frontier Tale" at Various Locations
16	Ridge Day Bicentennial Parade
16	St. Rita's Festival
17	Citizens Against Substance Abuse Bicentennial Celebrity Banquet at Sheraton Springdale
18	Charity Golf Tournament at Beckett Ridge CC
18	Opening Night of Summer Days - Norwood
22	Soccer–US Olympic Team Exhibition at Galbraith Field

22-24	Windjammers Circus Concert Band at Florence Mall, Oldenberg Brewery and Corbett Auditorium/UC
23, 27, 29	"On the Banks" at Bicentennial Commons, Seasongood Pavilion and Mt. St. Joseph
29 & 30	Cincinnati Riverfront Stadium Festival

A U G U S T

3, 5-7, 13, 14	"A Frontier Tale" at Various Locations
3-7	Hamilton County Fair
3-7	Community Panels Traveling Exhibit at Hamilton County Fair
13	A Day in Eden - Eden Park
13-14 15-21	Thriftway ATP Championship at Kings Island Qualifying Events Championship Events
20, 21	The Great Inland Seafood Festival '88 at Serpentine Wall
26-28	NIP Magazine Bicentennial Business, Cultural and International Hair Fashion Exposition at Convention Center
29-Oct. 8	"Hidden Treasures" – An Exhibition of Riches from the Greater Cincinnati Consortium of Colleges & Universities at Public Library

S E P T E M B E R

Sept.-Oct	Bicentennial Quilt on Display at Bicentennial Reception Center
1-25	Bicentennial Exhibit at Sharon Woods
2-Nov. 29	Giant Panda Exhibit at Cincinnati Zoo
5	Riverfest '88 - Riverfront
6-10	World Championship of Disc Golf at Hamilton County Parks
8-18	1988 Cincinnati Theatre Festival
9-11	Oktoberfest '88/10th Anniversary at MainStasse
9-Oct. 22	Cincinnati ReView at Images Gallery
11	Bicentennial Tour of Cathedral - St. Peter in Chains Cathedral
16	Friends of the William Howard Taft Birthplace Public Dinner at The Phoenix
16-17	The Bicentennial International Chess Challenge at Westin Atrium
16-18	Oktoberfest-Zinzinnati - Fifth Street, Downtown
17	Cincinnati Bicentennial Mayor's Cup Regatta at Public Landing
17	William Howard Taft Birthplace Grand Opening
22	"A Night at the Races" at Turfway Park

24	A Bicentennial Charity Ball Fashion Show at Hyatt Regency
24	Cincinnati Court Dancers at Art Museum
24	Miami/UC 100th Anniversary Game at Yager Stadium, Miami University
24-25	Taste of Blue Ash '88 - Blue Ash Towne Square
25	"River Crossings" at Music Hall
25	Columbia-Tusculum Historic Homes Tour

O C T O B E R

1	River Relay Race/Riverwalk Dedication - Riverfront: Cincinnati, Covington, Newport
1 2	Cincinnati Railroad Club Muncie Flyer Excursion Train Trip Bluegrass Limited Excursion Train Trip
2	Bicentennial Carnival: "A Taste of Carthage"
6	"To Cincinnati With Love Gala" from the Black Fashion & Beauty Community at Convention Center
9	Fire Museum Chili Festival
9	Dayton Street Historic District House Tour
10-21	"Quilts with a Cincinnati Connection: 200 Years of the Tradition" at Chiquita Center
13-16	Tall Stacks - Riverfront
14	Lite Up Cincinnati - Downtown
14-16	23rd Annual Cincinnati Antiques Festival at Music Hall Ballroom
14-Dec. 31	Bicentennial Furniture Exhibition at Carew Towers Arcade
15	Sharon JoAnn Moss Bicentennial Gala at Convention Center
15-16	Kentucky World Organization of China Painters at Radisson Inn
22	Cincinnati Flyers Bicentennial Wheelchair Basketball Game at Lloyd High School
23	Lecture by Dr. Hubertus Falkner Von Sonnenburg to Initiate "Masterworks from Munich" at Art Museum
25-Jan. 8	"Masterworks from Munich: 16th-18th Century Paintings from the Alte Pinakothek" at Art Museum
27-29	Cincinnati Ballet Presents: "Rosalinda" at Music Hall
29	Ribbon Cutting Ceremony at Fountain Square Dan Beard Boy Scout Riverwalk Trail Dedication of Boy Scout Plaza - Covington
30	Bicentennial Music Festival/Choir Festival at St. Peter in Chains Cathedral

N O V E M B E R

5	"Focus: 88–The Black Artist" Exhibition at Contemporary Arts Center
6	Visual Arts Exhibition at Contemporary Arts Center "Goin' Up Yonder" Dance Performance at Taft High School
6	Bicentennial Music Festival/UC CCM Brass Choir at St. Peter in Chains Cathedral
7	Visual Arts Exhibition at Contemporary Arts Center
9	Concert of the German Ensemble "Trio Basso" at Patricia Corbett Theatre/UC
13	Bicentennial Music Festival/A Vocal Arts Ensemble at St. Peter in Chains Cathedral
16, 30	Lectures on "Masterworks from Munich" at Art Museum
18	"Volunteerism & Citizen Expectations for the City's Third Century" Forum at Clarion
18-20	International Folk Festival at Convention Center
18-20	Salzsieders Dancers from Germany at Convention Center
19, 20, 25-27	Winterfest at Kings Island
20	Isaac Wise Temple Presents a Historical Overview of Reformed Jewish Music at Plum Street Temple
26	A Bicentennial Charity Ball at Clarion
26 & 27	Thanksgiving in Sharon Woods Village

D E C E M B E R

2-31	Winterfest at Kings Island
2, 3, 4, 9, 10, 11	Christmas in the Village at Sharon Woods
3-Jan. 3	Festival of Lights at Cincinnati Zoo
9	Christmas Display at Krohn Conservatory
14	Lectures on "Masterworks from Munich" at Art Museum
24/25	Christmas Masses with Hymns & Carols by Cincinnati Composers at St. Peter in Chains
26	"Black Cincinnati: Journey Across Time" Reception & Dinner at Omni Netherland Plaza
27	"Black Cincinnati: Journey Across Time" A Symposium on the Black Experience in Cincinnati at Omni Netherland Plaza
28	The Bicentennial Birthday at Convention Center
31	Great American Broadcasting Countdown '89 - Downtown

CONTRIBUTORS

The celebration of Cincinnati's bicentennial year was certainly an impressive feat. The imagination and perseverance of Commission staff members, the unfaltering dedication of thousands of volunteers, and the support of Ohio and Kentucky governmental bodies created a near-perfect recipe for an unforgettable 200th birthday bash.

Still, the main ingredient must be added to ensure success: the corporate contributors.

In 1984, it was rather difficult to convince potential "investors" that their contributions were needed for an event not yet planned. But suppliers of goods and services came forth to establish an efficient office environment and to support Commission operations.

Each annual report, newsletter, brochure, audio-visual presentation and piece of stationery was donated. Every word processor, electronic typewriter, desk, chair, cup of coffee and the copy machine was the gift of a contributing company. And each of the programs, major events and capital improvement projects dedicated during 1988 was the result of corporate contributions.

Therefore, the following list of bicentennial contributors is a vivid reflection of what gives Cincinnati its bold spirit. It is an inspiring blend of individuals and small businesses, governments and international corporations which gave above and beyond to invest in the city's future. They made so many dreams come true.

If space allowed, the names of 5,000 volunteers would also be listed, for they, too, were bicentennial contributors. Cincinnati has gained national recognition for its remarkable, professional volunteer force. The bicentennial year is yet another example of how the community benefits from the active involvement of these men and women who dedicated so much of their time and talents.

These two bodies are the true heroes of the bicentennial. Hopefully, each of those individuals and businesses which gave of themselves on this historic occasion will continue to receive the community recognition and appreciation they so richly deserve.

APPLAUSE!

C O N T R I B U T O R S

Official Sponsor ($200,000 +) American Financial Corporation Cincinnati Bell Cincinnati's Brewery, Hudepohl-Schoenling City of Cincinnati Community Mutual Blue Cross &
Cincinnati Pontiac Pacesetters Great American Broadcasting Company Great American Insurance Company The Greater Cincinnati Foundation Hamilton County Board of Commiss
Company Robert H Reakirt Foundation Harold C. Schott Foundation Star Bank N.A. Cincinnati State of Ohio Thriftway Food.Drugs United Dairy Farmers Channel 5, WLWT-
1230AM-WDJO WIZF-RADIO WKRC-RADIO WKRQ-FM WLLT-FM WMLX-Amber Broadcasting WWEZ-FM **Proud Patron ($25,000 - $199,000)** American Society of Landscap
Corporation Bentley Meisner Associates, Inc. CSX Transportation, Inc. Cavalier Audio-Visual Central Investment Corporation The Central Trust Company, N.A. Cincinnati Bus
America Deloitte, Haskins + Sells Deluxe Engraving Eric Doepke Associates Drawbridge Inn - Oldenberg Brewery The Drees Company R. C. Durr Company, Inc. Eagle-Picher In
Financial Services Greater Cincinnati Convention & Visitors Bureau Richard Goettle Inc. William Guentter & Son, Inc. Dr. Frederick A. Hauck Mr. & Mrs. Robert Heimann The H
Inc. Lawler Ballard Advertising LaRosa's Pizzerias Lewis-Shane CPA Mann & Bukvic Associates Martiny & Company McDonald's of Greater Cincinnati Meier's Wine Cellars, Inc.
Construction Company Multimedia Broadcasting Company National Endowment for the Humanities NS Group, Inc./Newport Steel & Imperial Adhesives The Nielsen Lithographing
Life Insurance Company F. J. O'Neill Charitable Contribution Patrick Media Group, Inc. Mr. & Mrs. Bradford E. Phillips Promotions With Results Quantum Chemical Corporation Jo
Inc. Skyline Chili, Inc. Jack J. Smith, Jr. Charitable Trust Smith-Kaufman Public Relations Steelcraft Building Products Mr. & Mrs. Joseph S. Stern, Jr. Stockton West Burkhart, Inc
Corporation UPDATE of Cincinnati, Inc. University of Cincinnati Mr. & Mrs. Michael D. Valentine Velva-Sheen Manufacturing Company Albert W. Vontz The Ronald F. Walker Family
Wolf & Sons, Inc. 19XIX Xavier University Arthur Young Young & Klein, Inc. Zender + Associates, Inc. **Contributor ($5,000 - $24,999)** AD.EX Inc. Alco Building Products
Riverboats, Inc. Barleycorn's The Barr Foundation Bartlett & Company Bausch Brothers Masonry Baxter Concrete Products, Inc. Beckman, Weil, Shepardson & Faller Benesch,
Subsidiary of Aluma Systems Mr. & Mrs. Barrett Buse Mr. & Mrs. Raymond Buse, Jr. Business-Expo Business Information Storage, Inc. Mr. & Mrs. Owen B. Butler Mr. & M
Masons Chase Bank of Ohio Cincinnati Art Museum Cincinnati Equitable Insurance Company Cincinnati Historical Society Cincinnati Institute of Fine Arts Cincinnati Microwa
Association Clarion Hotel J. D. Cloud & Company Comey & Shepherd, Inc. Complete Systems, Inc. Contemporary Arts Center Coopers & Lybrand Cope Audio The Corbett Founc
Corporation Deluxe Check Printers, Inc. Detales Imprinted Garments, Inc. Didier Taylor Refractories Corporation Dinsmore & Shohl Walter P. Dolle Insurance Agency, Inc. The Do
Company, Inc. C. Eberle & Sons Company Ebner & Riker Company, LPA Erlanger Lumber Company Ewing Industries, Inc. Fabritec International Fetter Printing Findlay Architect
Mallinckrodt, Inc. Frost & Jacobs GPA Technical Consultants, Inc. Tom Gaither Gem Savings Association Glaser Associates, Inc. Globe Business Interiors Globe Furniture Galleri
Cincinnati Building Owners and Managers Association Greater Cincinnati Chamber of Commerce The Greater Cincinnati White Castle Restaurants Dr. Michael A. Grefer Richard F.
Nolan & Stites Mr. & Mrs. Lanny Holbrook L. J. Hooker Developments Hopple Plastics, Inc. Hunt Development Corporation Huntington Banks Image Matrix, Inc. Interior Wooc
Company K Mart Corporation Kappen Excavating Company, Inc. Katz, Teller, Brant and Hild Mr. & Mrs. William J. Keating Keating, Muething & Klekamp Kenton County Airport Bc
Brown, Inc. Mr. & Mrs. Ralph Lazarus Leadership Cincinnati Alumni Association Legg Mason Wood Walker, Inc. Mr. & Mrs. William N. Liggett M B S Associates, Inc. Mc Alpin's Mc
Systems Marsh & McLennan Incorporated Mayerson Associates May Festival Association Mayfield Neurological Institute Merit Savings Association Frank Messer & Sons Const
Conference of Christians and Jews Nationwide Paper Mr. & Mrs. Louis Nippert Nutone, Division/Scovil Ogden Food Services State of Ohio, Arts Council State of Ohio, Humani
Incorporated Peat, Marwick, Main & Company Pease Industries J. C. Penney Co. The Perry & Derrick Company Mr. & Mrs. Daniel Pfau Mr. & Mrs. David C. Phillips Phoenix F
Co. Mr. & Mrs. C. Lawson Reed Rendigs, Fry, Kiely & Dennis Reynolds, Dewitt & Company Richards Industries Richardson & Associates, Inc. Ms. Rebecca Richardson Robinson
Associates The Santangelo Group Mr. & Mrs. John Sawyer Joseph W. Scherr, Jr. Schiff, Kriedler-Shell, Inc. Schmidlapp Park Fund Schumacher Dugan Construction Company Se
District Council of Carpenters South-Western Publishing Company Southwestern Ohio Education Association Space Design International Inc. St. Elizabeth Medical Center Standarc
Tassian Organization, Inc. The Telephone Pioneers of America The Terrace Hilton totes, Incorporated Triangle Productions Turner Construction Company U.S. Precision Lens The
Chesley Co./Stanley M. Chesley Walgreens Warner Amex Cable Communications, Inc. The Waterfront Westhorn Company Westpac Banking Corporation Robert and Ruth Westh
Communications Corporation Xtek, Inc. Zayre Corporation The C. W. Zumbiel Company Mr. & Mrs. Robert W. Zumbiel **Official Supplier ($10,000 + in goods and**
Co. Barkan/Keeling/Taggart Photography, Inc. Carey Color Inc./Cincinnati Cincinnati Bell Long Distance Cincinnati Competitors Coffee Break Services, Inc. COMAIR, Inc. Concep
Productions, Inc. Duro Bag Manufacturing Company Eastman Kodak Company Elder Photographic, Inc. Encore Production Services George E. Fern Company Robert Flischel
Inc. Hamilton Sorter Company Gus Holthaus Signs, Inc. The Home City Ice Co. ITA Inc., Industrial Training Aids Johnston Paper Company Pre-Press Service, Inc. QC Type Inc.
Works Small Business Data Processing Corporation Smith Photography Something Different Interior Plantscaping Spectrum Map Publishing Co., Inc. Tourcrafters, Inc. Typo-S
Brothers AIR Studio Airborne Express Airborne Specialty Advertising & Promotions Mark Alexander Robert H. Allen Allied Construction Industries Alpha Delta Boule of Sigma
Company Mr. & Mrs. Ronald Anderson Apcoa Arab Association Architects Sales, Inc. Architectural Metal Erectors, Inc. Arnco Printing Arnold Printing Arrow Blue Company Ar
Company Gordon Baer W.J. Baker Company, Inc. Dr. & Mrs. E. David Ballard Balloons Across the River Bankhardt's, Inc. BASF Corporation, Inmont Division Baxter, Hodell, Donn
Mrs. Theodore M. Berry Bethesda Hospital, Inc. Helen Black Dr. Stanley Block B'nai Tzedek Sisterhood Bode Finn Company Judith Bogart The Bolce Paint Company Bonnie Ly
Co. Bullard Company Congressman Jim Bunning Burgess & Niple, Ltd. Henry Burton Busken Bakeries Tom Butscha, Inc. C.B.C. Erectors, Inc. C.H.C. Fabricators Corporation
Choir Cellular One Centennial Savings & Loan Company Central Business Systems & Security Concepts Central Steel & Wire Company Mr. & Mrs. William Chambers John D. C
Company Cheviot Building & Loan Co. Chevron USA, Inc. Children's Hospital Medical Center Chinese American Association Christ Hospital Cincinnati Air Conditioning Cinci
Company Cincinnati Consulting Engineers, Inc. Cincinnati Dental Society Cincinnati Fire Museum Cincinnati Gear Company Cincinnati Junior Strings Cincinnati Mack Sales & Servic
Orchestra Cincinnati Technical College Cincinnati Time, Inc. Cincinnati Union Bethel The Cincinnati Woman's Club Cincinnati Women's Forum Cincinnati Word Processing Cincom
Cohen & Sons, Inc. Cold Spring Millwork Coldwell Banker Commercial Real Estate Services Colonial Ad Products, Inc. Colonial Dames of America Commonwealth Hilton Cor
Inc. Corinthian Woodworking Donald Corken Covenant Philanthea Class - Covenant First Presbyterian Church Cover Up's Covington-Cincinnati Suspension Bridge Committee Create
Company Diversified Communications Dobson The Mover Mr. & Mrs. John S. Domaschko Robert W. Dorsey Downtown Council Mr. & Mrs. Marc Dragul Daniel Drake Memorial
Edwards Jim Effler Myretta & Norman Egner Ehmke Movers, Inc. Eleftherios Karkadoulias City of Elsmere, Kentucky Eppa Rixey Agency Inc. Electro-Jet Tool and Manufacturing
Equipment Co. F & W Publications, Inc. Kelly Farrish Faultless Bakeries Fechheimer Brothers Company Federated Garden Club of Cincinnati and Vicinity Mr. & Mrs. Mark Feldn
Associates Edward J. Flesch Flying Tigers Barbara H. Ford City of Fort Mitchell, Kentucky City of Fort Thomas, Kentucky Fosdick & Hilmer Mr. & Mrs. Stanley E. Foster Founta
Division/Emerson Electric Company FYRE-FYTER Sales & Service Rev. John D. Gaines Gamco, Inc. Lynn Garcia Gardner Publications Garfield Electric, Inc. Donald E. Garro
Go Graham-Obermeyer & Partners, Ltd. Gravure Systems G.A. Gray Company Great American Chocolate Cookie Co., Inc. Greater Cincinnati Beautiful, Inc. Greater Cincinnati In
Hardware, Inc. Hamilton County Council American Legion Auxiliary Ray Hamilton Company Hamilton Mutual Insurance Company Hancock Textile Company Sister Jean F
Hendricks Herbert-Verkamp-Calvert Chemical Company Hilltop Research, Inc. Hillman Fasteners HI-LO Climbers Hixson Architects/Engineers John & Nancy Hobstetter Mrs. Mine
Hub, P.S.C. Hulefeld Associates Ben Hur Construction Company, Inc. Pete Huster Hyde Park Square Business Association Hydro Systems Company Ilsco Division - Bardes Corp
Inc. JMB/Federated Realty Associates, Ltd. J & S Lithography B & J Jacobs Co. Robert James Company, Inc. Japanese American Citizens League Rev. & Mrs. Andrew Jerge
Corporation Kenwood Garden Club Kenwood Woman's Club Mr. & Mrs. David H. King J. T. King & Company King Container Service A. M. Kinney, Inc. KIRIGAMI Klingenberg
Group F. D. Lawrence Electric Co. Lawyers Title of Cincinnati, Inc. LeBlond Makino Machine Tool Company Le Cercle Francois de Cuite Legge Associates, Inc. Lewin Monument
Center Lorenz and Williams Loth, Inc. Kenneth R. Lucas Houston L. Lumpkin, III, M.D. Lutheran Church of the Good Shepherd Lynch Fish Company Madeira PEO Sisterhood Ch
Inc. Anita Marks - Design Matthew United Church of Christ Mayers Electric Media That Works, Inc. Meierjohan-Wengler, Inc. Mellott & Mellott Mercer-Meidinger-Hansen,
Contractors Middle-West Concrete Forming & Equipment Co. Charles A. Miller & Sons, Inc. Earl B. Miller Co., Inc. Jeff Miller Miller, Myers & Associates Mr. & Mrs. C. E. Mi
Inc. Mosler, Inc. Mound Steel Corporation Mt. Washington Wagon Wheels Mueller/Reading Rock Frederick P. Murdock & Company Mutual of America National Flag Compar
Choir Nivison-Weiskopf Company Norfolk Southern Corporation North College Hill Bake Shop Northern Kentucky Chamber of Commerce Northern Kentucky Restaurant Associat
Corporation Olsten of Cincinnati, Inc. Omer Foods, Inc. Omnigraphics Open Systems, Inc. Marilyn A. Ormsbee The Osborne Coinage Company Mr. & Mrs. Herbert E. Ostrov Our La
Orthopaedic Associates, Inc. Peoples Liberty Bank of Northern Kentucky Mr. & Mrs. Keith Peterson Thomas E. Petry Phloxy Ladies Garden Club Photo Lab, Inc. Photo Posters Dan
Dispatch Prince Reproductions Printers Bindery Process Construction, Inc. Production Plaza Professional Data Resources Project Skills Providence/St. Francis-St. George Hospital
Securities Queen City Woman's Club Queensgate Press Mr. & Mrs. Robert A. Quisno R.E.L. Enterprises, Inc. R & K Group Mr. & Mrs. Gary Rabiner Louis L. Rauh Reams Co
Company Dr. & Mrs. George Rieveschl, Jr. Rochford Kennedy & Company Rolling Pin Pastry Company Michael D. Rose B. J. Rowekamp & Son Ruder Finn & Rothman, Inc. R. Ru
Company Safeco Insurance Companies Robert B. Sathe J. Sawyer Company Ruth D. Sawyer Rastislav R. Sayers Mr. & Mrs. John Scahill Schauer Manufacturing Corporation
Inc. Seco Electric Selby Service, Roxy Press, Inc. Senco Products Serta of Ohio Servatti Pastry Shops Seven Hills Savings Association Robert and Becky Shaffer Marcia Shortt Sh
& Rowekamp Snits Mr. & Mrs. Eric Soovere Southern Ohio Fabricators City of Southgate, Kentucky Spaulding Lighting City of Springdale Spring Grove Sheet Metal Co. Square
Loan Funding Corporation Studio Art Services Sun Chemical Corporation Super Food Services Swallen's Inc. Swiss Benevolent Society Symons Corp. T & W Printing Taft Museu
Associates Thomas Moore College Kampus Kats Henry P. Thompson Company James H. Thompson Funeral Home, Inc. The Timers Club Tipton Associates, Inc. Tom Walker Tishey
River Division Robert F. Uhrig Company United Italian Society of Greater Cincinnati United Methodist Women, W.H.A. University of Cincinnati - DAAP University of Cincinnati -
Wachs Wagner Repro & Supply Co. Waldenbooks Walker & Company, Inc. Tom Walker Walnut Garage Tony Walsh Geoffrey Warneford Mr. & Mrs. Sidney Weil Wellington Corpor
& Mrs. John Whitehurst Widmer's Cleaners Wilkinson Enterprises Wilson & Associates T. H. Winston Company Woman's Auxiliary of Winton Place Women's Guild Matthew United Chur

ederated Department Stores Inc. and Lazarus The Fifth Third Bank/The Schmidlapp Foundation General Electric Foundation General Motors Corporation-Pontiac Division Greater
Food Systems, Inc. Kahn's & Company Kentucky Fried Chicken Corporation The Kroger Company The Procter & Gamble Company The Provident Bank The Prudential Property
ati Enquirer The Cincinnati Post Jacor Communications/WEBN/700WLW Scripps Howard/WCPO-TV FM105-WUBE WARM-98FM WBLZ-FM WBVE-FM WCIN-Radio WCKY-AM
neriTrust Co. N.A. Amity Unlimited, Inc. Arthur Andersen & Co. Ashland Oil Foundation, Inc. Avon Products, Inc. L.S. Ayres & Company Baker Concrete Construction, Inc. Belcan
Cincinnati Financial Corporation The Cincinnati Gas & Electric Company Cincinnati Magazine Cincinnati Milacron, Inc. Cintas Corporation Dan Beard Council Boy Scouts of
he Thomas J. Emery Memorial James E. Evans Family Ferguson Van Lines, Inc./Ferguson Moving & Storage Freedman Advertising Frisch's Big Boy Gannett Foundation Gradison
any Hyatt Regency Cincinnati IBM Corporation The David J. Joseph Company KZF Incorporated Mr. & Mrs. Robert T. Keeler Kenner Products, Division of Kenner Parker Toys,
armaceuticals, Inc. Merrill Lynch, Pierce, Fenner & Smith, Inc. Meyers/Lohnes Agency-The Equitable Financial Companies The Midland Company Miller-Valentine Group Monarch
nern Kentucky Convention & Visitors Bureau Norton Outdoor Advertising State of Ohio, Department of Development State of Ohio, Department of Natural Resources Ohio National
Russell Charitable Trust The Sawyer Place Company Schenker, Probst + Barensfeld Louise Taft Semple Foundation Seven-Up/Royal Crown Bottling Co. Shearson Lehman Hutton,
Stores/Hook-Super-X Inc. Taft, Stettinius & Hollister Philip Taliaferro III Ticketmaster Corporation of Ohio Matth. Toebben Construction Co. Towne Properties, Ltd. The U.S. Shoe
/GUC-FM West Shell, Inc. The Western-Southern Life Insurance Company The Westin Hotel Wilder-Fearn & Associates Winegardner & Hammons, Inc. & Cincinnati Holiday Inns H.
erican Institute of Architects AT&T Architectural Foundation of Cincinnati William D. Atteberry Automanage, Inc. Automatic Data Processing, Inc. The G. A. Avril Company B B
land & Aronoff Berman Printing Company The Bernstein Family bigg's Boone County, Kentucky Brandenburg, Carroll & Farrish Bressler & Company SAMI/Burke, Inc. Burke, A
ler Carlisle Companies, Incorporated Carlisle Construction Company, Inc. Castellini Company Catt Lyon Design The Ceco Corporation Central Trust, Northern Kentucky Cement
nati Museum of Natural History Cincinnati Rowing Center Cincinnati Town & Country Garden Club The Cincinnati Zoo Cindus Corporation Citizens Federal Savings and Loan
x Companies City of Covington Crescent Paper Tube Company, Inc. R. C. Crisler & Co., Inc. The Crosset Family Fund Kenneth Cunningham & Associates Data Processing Sciences
To Door Transportation Services Downing Displays The Drackett Company Dravo Basic Materials, Inc. Dubois/Chemed Corporation Duncan Hines/Crisco Oil Eaton Asphalt Paving
Inc. City of Florence, Kentucky Ford Motor Company, Batavia - UAW Local 863 Formica Corporation Four Seasons Garment Company Franklin Savings Fries & Fries Division of
Charles W. Goering Gold Star Chili Graeter's, Inc. Grant Thornton, Accountants and Management Consultants Graphitti Studios Larry Grause Graydon, Head & Ritchey Greater
ill Robert Grove Harlan Typographic The Frank Herschede Company Hilltop Basic Resources Hilton-Davis Chemical Company Gerald D. Hines Interests Mr. William Hofler Hogan
national Business Exposition Jackson/Ridey & Company Janell, Inc. The Andrew Jergens Company R. A. Jones & Co., Inc. The Junior League of Cincinnati John R. Jurgensen
unty, Kentucky The Kentucky Post Kentucky National Bank Kersten Estate Ms. Page Kess Kings Productions Kelly Kolar Design Jay Korte Krienik & Associates, Inc. Landrum &
Andrew B. McLandrich Mr. & Mrs. Jack Maier MainStrasse Village Association The Maisonette Group J. Malsh & Company Manhattan Life Insurance Company Manticore Sound
chel & Sons Construction Midland Enterprises, Inc. Mr. & Mrs. Lloyd I. Miller Mutual Manufacturing & Supply Company National City Bank National City Corporation National
io Valley Carpenters Joint Apprenticeship Committee The Ohio Valley Foundation Ohio Valley Quilters' Guild Omni Netherland Plaza PDT + Company Architects/Planners PKG's
orporation Plastic Moldings Company Elissa May Plattner Port Authority of Cincinnati & Hamilton County Price Waterhouse Queen City Metro Dan Ransohoff Frederick Rauh &
and Wentz, P.S.C. Rotex, Inc. The Rotary Club of Cincinnati Mr. & Mrs. William S. Rowe Rubloff Institutional Services Ryerson Steel Saks Fifth Avenue Robert E. Sanders and
Co. Seasongood & Mayer Sena Weller Rohs & Williams Inc. SENCORP Sibcy Cline Siebert Design Small Business Data Processing Corporation C. Smith Studios Southwest Ohio
ardust Productions Mr. & Mrs. John J. Strader Strauss & Troy The George Strike Family Suburban Federal Savings & Loan Taliaferro and Mann The Talking Yellow Pages George
Life Insurance Company United Air Specialists, Inc. Van Leunens Mr. & Mrs. William G. Verst Vorys, Sater, Seymour and Pease Mr. C. Gordon Wade Waite, Schneider, Bayless &
Mrs. Harris K. Weston Williamsburg of Cincinnati The Williamson Company The Witt Company Thomas E. Wood, Inc. Woolpert Consultants Jeff Wyler Dealer Group, Inc. Xenas
right Cincinnati, Inc. Ameritech Mobile Communications Sales Amko Plastics, Inc. Apple Computer Art Woodworking & Manufacturing Company Baldwin Piano & Organ
cations Cincinnati Cordage & Paper Company CNW Printing, Inc./Colour, Inc. Curtis Duplication Display Sales, Inc. Dorl and Fern Florist The David Douglas Corporation Downie
Four Seasons Garment Company France/Walsh Photography Jeff Friedman Photography The Future Now The Gap, Inc. Gentry Shops Gerrior Photography Gibson Greetings,
mousine Service RDI Marketing Services, Inc. RTG Music Robin Color Lab, Inc. S. Rosenthal & Company Rozzi's Famous Fireworks Scot Business Machines Co. Sidney Printing
T. Verdin Company Wolf Photography **Friend (Under $5,000)** Acme Wrecking Co., Inc. ADT Security Systems Addison Clipson Architects, Inc. Advertisers' Club Aglamesis
ity American Airlines American Isowall Corporation American Micro Products, Inc. American Sign & Marketing Services Ammon Nursery Annie Anderson Anderson Publishing
Associated Irish Organizations of Greater Cincinnati Association Administrators Atlas Dry Cleaners AudioCraft Recording Company Melinda Auge & Associates Augur Tool & Die
nc. Beckett Paper Company Dale Benedict Bernie Beck Consulting Bedinghaus Business Forms Company Bell & Hortenstine City of Bellevue, Kentucky Bennett Ford Sales Mr. &
onomini Bakeries Dr. Leon E. Boothe Brentwood Savings Association Meem Breyer Brighton Corporation Brinck & Schmidt, Inc. Buckeye School Pictures Robert W. Bugie Sales
neral Caporale Photography Carmargo Bakery Carthage School 4th Graders John E. Carrigan Plumbing Co. Susan F. Castellini The Cathedral Basilica Of The Assumption Adult
ter Y, PEO Sisterhood Charter Bus Service & Klug School Bus Service Chase Family Foundation William Rowell Chase Henry H. Chatfield Chavez Properties, Inc. Chelsea Moore
Club Cincinnati Armature Works, Inc. Cincinnati Art Academy Cincinnati Automobile Club Cincinnati Builders Supply Co. Cincinnati Carver's Guild Cincinnati Concrete Pipe
Mortgage Bankers Association Cincinnati Reds Cincinnati School of Court Reporting The Cincinnati Steel Products Company Cincinnati Steel Treating Company Cincinnati Symphony
flow Products, Inc. Clarity Systems Dr. R. E. Clark Tony Clark Clark, Schaefer, Hackett & Company The Clay Factory Clean Cincinnati, Inc. Clopay Corporation Cobb Type Mose
seph T. Condit Joseph Connaughton Consulate General of the Federal Republic of Germany Contemporary Galleries, Inc. Controlled Credit Corporation Copper & Brass Sales,
ve Company Darke County Lightning Protection, Inc. Deaconess Hospital Don Demming Derringer Food Services, Inc. Designer Services Group Andrew Devlin Diem & Wing Paper
& Bradstreet Credit Services Lucille Durrell Dyment Company Eckert Welding Company, Inc. Edge Graphics, Inc. City of Edgewood, Kentucky Educational Services Institute Tom
. Environmental Land Development Association Ernst & Whinney Estonian Americans Ray Evers Welding Company Executone of Cincinnati George Eyrich F & M Group - MAFCO
gging Company M. K. Ferguson Company Fetes De Jeunesse Fibre Glass Evercoat, Inc. Fine Arts Fund Mike Fink Restaurant Finite Company Christopher P. Finney E. J. Finney
d.e. Foxx & Associates Foxx & Company Foy-Johnston, Inc. Frame King John J. Frantz Friemark, Inc. Friends of Covington Friends of Kenton County Library Frye Signs Fusite
al Foods Corporation Julie Boudousquie Gerdsen German American Citizens Group Lucas Girling - Truck Brake Division Good Samaritan Hospital Margot Gotoff Gourmet To
urance Jeff Green Mr. & Mrs. John B. Greene Greiwe Interiors Jeff Grimes Groenke Organization Richard Grogan Grote Bakeries Charles Grund Dr. Joe N. Hackworth Hader
gton Harrison Home Bakery Hartford Insurance Group Harvey Brothers Amy Heinichen Paul Hemmer Construction Henderson & Bodwell Henderson Music Company Ted
mer Patrick Hogan Hoge, Warren-Zimmerman Company Jesse J. Holland Home Builders Association Horst Colorlab, Inc. Martin J. Horwitz Mr. & Mrs. John Hrebenyar William
Association of Greater Cincinnati International Paper Company Interpersonal Communications Associates IRS Training & Development Iron Workers Local Union No. 44 J.H.H.,
ptist Church The Jewish Hospital Johnson Electric Supply Company Johnson Group Management Johnson & Higgins of Ohio, Inc. Bertha Lacy Jones Ronald G. Joseph Jung
& Mrs. John Knochelman Koopers-Walker-Williams Lumber Korb Check Printers, Inc. Mr. & Mrs. Carl A. Kroch Ron Lally Dr. Clarence E. Lamb, Jr. Matthew Jay Lane Latvian
ne D. Lewis The Licking-Riverside Neighborhood Association Linclay Corporation Line For Line, Inc. The Lithuanian Group of Cincinnati Little Dutch Bakery Longworth Hall Design
scher and Company Main Auction Galleries, Inc. Jon Malis MarketVision J. L. Marshall News Company McSwain Carpets Robert G. McGraw & Company Management Design,
Homes, Inc. Mercury Instruments The Merten Company Metcut Research Associates Metro Instant Press The Metzger Machine Company Chuck Meyer Middendorf-Niehoff
t-It, Inc. Ralph F. Mitchell Modern Machinery Company Montgomery Women's Club Morning Star Baptist Church Mortgage Bankers of Greater Cincinnati Moskowitz Brothers,
ndscape Organization, Inc. Paul Louis Neff James A. Nelson Mr. & Mrs. Richard Nelson Newman Brothers, Inc. City of Newport, Kentucky Ninth Street Baptist Inspirational
Porsche Audi Northwest Paper Company H. C. Nutting Company OKI Systems Daniel Oates O'Connor & Klein, Inc. Ohio Hydraulics, Inc. Ohio Valley Supply Company Ohmart
Hospital Pagemakers Paine Webber, Inc. Antonio Palazzolo Company Mr. & Mrs. Thomas Patterson C.M. Paula Company Paxton Lumber Company Paxton & Seasongood Pediatric
neer Antique and Hobby Association PIP Printing Plainville Concrete Plastigraphics, Inc. Polish American Society of Greater Cincinnati R. L. Polk Company Portion Pac, Inc. Priority
e & Accident Insurance Company Public Library of Cincinnati and Hamilton County Bob Pulte Oldsmobile, Inc. Judith Pultz Quality Typesetting Queen City Blacktop Co. Queen City
constructive Orthopedics Red Bank Transport, Inc. Regina Bakeries Remke's Markets Bakery Mr. & Mrs. Joseph Rettig James B. Reynolds Kumbert Richter Riemeier Lumber
. John Runyan Rusk Heating & Air Conditioning Ruthman Machinery Company SHV Real Estate St. Catherine's Women Society St. Joseph Church St. Pius Church Saalfeld Paper
Schiff W. F. Schildman Earl D. Schilling Schonberg Associates Schottenstein Stores Howard Schultz & Associates Central States, Inc. Michael Schuster & Associates Sealtron,
ews Corporation Siemens Energy & Automation, Inc. Tom Sigafoos Singer Wallpaper & Paint Sive Associates, Inc. Slide Craft, Inc. Smith & Schnacke Smith, Wolnitzek, Schachter
Stearns Technical Textile Stevenson Photo Color Mr. & Mrs. David Stolberg Stone Center Carl A. Strauss & Associates Jerome Stricker Strickland & Wright Barry Strum Student
Society Charles S. Tappan E. H. Tassett Inc. Tate Building Supply Company Technical Equipment Sales Company Tepe, Hensler & Westerkamp, Inc. Textile Prints G. J. Thelan &
ay Line of Cincinnati Tressa, Inc. Trinity United Church of God Tri-Tex Company Trius Products Kendall Trotter Tuesday Club/Knox Presbyterian U.S. Army Corps of Engineers - Ohio
are Books Dept. Valvax Corporation J. Richard Verkamp The Vernon Manor Hotel Vieux Carre Photo Village Pantry Catering Virginia Bakery Vivi-Color, Inc. WNOP Radio Gary
Coal & Coke Company Welsh Society of Greater Cincinnati Wendling Printing Charles Westheimer Westwood Methodist Church Westwood Woman's Club Mr. & Mrs. Frank White Mr.
d Frank E. Wood Wood Graphics, Inc. Wood, Herron & Evans Wood & Lamping Mrs. John Wuslin Xerox Corporation Xomox Corporation Young & Bertke Sheet Metal Co. David Zinn

Publisher's Notes:

Production of this commemorative Bicentennial Review was only possible because of the total dedication of several individuals.

First and foremost to be recognized is Rick Greiwe. We all rode the crest of his wave prior to, throughout and now after the year '88. His tremendous enthusiasm coupled with efficient implementation was always tempered by a sensitivity to the people involved. This book is a monument to Rick's tireless efforts and his love affair with Cincinnati.

My special gratitude goes to Steve Dulle and his design firm Graphitti Studios. Steve has a genius for bringing beauty and practicality together on paper. He is flexible and solicitous when necessary, but devoted to his total concept of continuity and flow.

Steve's task was monumental. He produced layouts, set type, designed graphics, selected and sized photos, and made final art for our 160 page book in record time. His heart is in this book and it shows! The finished product is no doubt a review of '88, but every section subtly conveys Steve's sensitivity and bold approach.

Kelly Kolar and Mary Lynn Ricks brought a special ingredient to the book as employees of the Bicentennial Commission for five years. Kelly oversaw the selection of our award-winning photographs, chosen from thousands which were taken by Cincinnati's finest photographers. She coordinated the total photographic effort and made invaluable contributions to the design of *Cincinnati '88*. Mary Lynn brought insight and poetic sensitivity to the book. Her creativity as a copywriter and her obvious love for the Commission's efforts made for an easy marriage of design and copy. Kelly and Mary Lynn both postponed lucrative careers in the Graphic Arts to work on *Cincinnati '88*. Thank you, ladies.

Cincinnati '88: The Bicentennial Year in Review is dedicated most of all to the twelve photographers who worked the entire year, uncompensated, simply for the love of their city and their art. The magnificent photographs in this book are only a sampling of their total effort. This book would not be in print had they not cooperated from start to finish. Surely these twelve people are deserving of good things to come. In deep appreciation to: Hal Barkan, John Keeling, Chris Taggart, Robert Flischel, Jeff Friedman, Maureen France, Tony Walsh, Bob Gerrior, Jeff Wolf, Brad Smith, Michael Bennington, and Willie Hudson.

Thanks to Doug Nichols for spearheading the marketing of the book and thanks to the craftsmen at Young & Klein Lithographers who toil over every printing job as though it was a REMBRANDT!

◆

Scott H. Nichols, President
Young & Klein, Inc.